Spectrum of Depthless Enthusiasm

Rayne Corbin

This paperback edition, independently published as
Rayne Corbin Books, first published August 2020.

ISBN: 978-1-0807-7747-1

CONTENTS

SPECTRUM OF DEPTHLESS ENTHUSIASM

1. Aspergic Tendencies in the Surreal World

Envisioning a Normal World

Attempting to imagine a normally intending world provokes the obvious question: what is normalcy or the Normal? Normalcy could be considered a genetic emergence of well-adjusted, abundant nature and confident, niche-bursting environments, or as social clarity within a self-contending, self-aware species privileged by an endless, unknown universe it loudly proclaims to be found and encouraging to the reverence of its kind.

Normal is genetic distribution as a memory of cumulative solutions of the past: a method of extension connected as a lifeblood to the docile properties of reality through regulated reworking of its fixed forces to advantage. It is the same as species learn functions in nature through the influences of perceptual beliefs on future emotive, bodily explorations. Within evolution, it is the search for betterment through solutions, the normalcy of survival within a created atmosphere of heredities and embedded, temporally enacted enrichments.

Normal is the perpetual, transitional reuse of an animated, evolved reality, and the continual surfacing of the present moment as a developing culmination of the past. It is light, wondrously absorbing and reflecting a vibrant reality of coalescing forces for life to surface and affix with advancing evolutionary explanations. It is gravity gently coaxing a speck of dust to the ground while held buoyant by the friction of soft, stilled air and the exchange of contact. It is the dust, a smallest exhibit of humankind's unenhanced observation, far-reaching in its inner forceful, complex and particle reality, intimate and vital to the impassioned, stimulated observer while occurring mostly beyond any spans of accessible attention.

The normal is a universe incredibly grown into the synchronized forces of existence within which life and consciousness might appear to ponder its fitted place within it. It is a diversity of mutually shared experiences and innumerable awarenesses bound by hereditary solutions over a spanning landscape.

Normalcy is a common ground mutually and temporally within all species since a distant beginning when a recently initiated life attached itself and began traveling the opportunities the mentoring forces of reality newly permitted it to divulge, with its puzzling, effectually textured surfaces to affix rightfully in the middle of an infinite nowhere within a newly disclosed creation of regulated imagination.

Normal is not actually finding this universe except as an observer of something which might never be measured in its totality: an observer barely comprehending the local setting of its personal beginning, identity and making beyond the utilized bodily and environmental tools of survival it has been given by an affording world and contented cosmos.

~~

An observer of the world might be normalized and designed by its evolutionary choices and the solutions it is biologically bound incapable of viewing or truly imagining the hidden workings of reality except incredulously as coincidental accident or wrought as a reshaped iconic discovery plucked like a colored petal from an associated environment. Normal is the behavioral trust in changeless self-interpretation as the conviction of survival; and in the depriving promise of further insight and sensitivity still to be found in a furthering, impending future.

Considering normal in the natural world obviously includes nonhumanity in all its eloquence as an innovative mountain of multidimensional bodies with emotive motivations, heightened sensitive and interested awarenesses. Humanity in a current state is a recent occurrence within and outside of nature and should not have been capable to endure the complexities of its evolutionary bloom without a hitherto established level of normalcy in genetics for stowing behavioral memories for countless improving species. This abundance of animated solutions was designed into the living environments they shaped through soliciting answers atop an introverted planet, within a boundless universe often misconstrued as the divinely inherited ownership of humanity.

Supposedly and permittable by an unrepresented, unwary and unguarded nature as a choice of explanation within reality to conceivably implement, this ownership allegedly permits its full consumption for the attempting benefit and growth of dominant successes for one winning species designed capable of its truer refinement accorded its capacity to overcome the natural world for an advancing winning posture.

Humanity would not exist in its current state without the established diversity of memorized solutions shared as a representation through the genera of life enclosing a planet in its rapt interpretations; and occurring within a universe as a normal, bounded state of overwhelming, willful attainment not intended to be ousted by a singularly provoked, overcoming species as a genuine truth of encumbered survival.

In the world of genetics, convergent genres of skilled traits within species, niches, environments, perceptions and enactions, all with complex emergent realities, there is range, deviation, unifying multiplicity, the merging and distribution of enabled solutions bound to the fixtures of the existence they evolved alongside, as well as complexities of yet unfound probabilities of answers, pitfalls and traps awaiting inside reality to be unveiled and sprung into the unsuspecting world as the compulsive drive swelling from the struggle for better universal elucidations.

Out of this same world appears playfulness, curiosity for its own sake, innovation and creativity for all species within divergent perceptual abilities and mental feats of invigorated, opined mysticisms.

Normalcy is balance, its fluidity observable in all facets of reality, in human-made science and religion, social politics, economics and overwhelmingly aligned alongside the natural world with its values and enforced fetters, and in the ongoing saga of human evolutionary confrontation with this poise of multilayered life through its many epochs of conflicted history.

The ebb and flow of eventful, coinciding histories reciprocally developing as betterment or deterioration through risky divergences from this illusive equilibrium or middle ground is the forceful struggle for a constancy of reality. This symmetry must exist in measure regardless of the actual perceived values of universal forces even if uneventful emptiness were the sole ruling force of the universe on a zero-sum scale. Without the vibrating deviations of a current existence permitting the affordances for advancing realms of extremism within the wide-ranging cosmos, there would be no possibility for life to surface as an otherworldly experience floating on a solar, frictional projection through a seemingly inert, benign emptiness, as an only technique affixing physical manifestations, and as an exclusion from an otherwise alternative stillness.

The underlaying delicacy of a symmetrical world made for diverse changes to merge into evolutionary paths, for the movements of life as an initial twitch to fatefully find and manifest as fruition within a flexible, shared, delimited and successful lifeforce tendrilled as countless temporal species bursting with bound genetic designs for the continuance of its allotted behavioral realization, the constancy of its flowing waters and energizing tides, its colorful, weathered and appeasing appearance, and its mountains of buried, hardened antiquity: a hard-fought multiplicity of answers permitting to occur the wilting current and previously wide spectrum of species as a collectively focused, cognizant state of reality on a planet.

Normal is the observation of equilibria at work in the natural world, as the innovations of survival for all species to disclose as awarenesses, valuations and skills of actions through the extremes of bound artistry reaping its predatory descriptions upon the suspecting, deeply enthusiastic and unbiased world.

~~

The spectacle of light from the continual rolling occurrence of the passive rising and setting sun on a rotating globe by a conscious species rooted to its place: endlessly, a circling maelstrom of locality is exposed to an inimitable sun's appearance and disappearance while capable of being deliberated or celebrated, temporally joined with every other spot on its surface based on the multifaceted, bloomed forces shaping its minor twirling occurrence within a nondisclosed speck of the universe. This spectacle of light and ledge of reality belongs to all species as a beginning and a budding source for uncovering symmetry to traverse the paths of life.

The original normalcy of reality and the natural world of species and forces can be irresistible for a newly conscious awareness to find itself attentive to as objects conquerable to its reachable courage; while held fixed to its originating locations as furthering, unravelling stories to widely expound.

This abruptness of discovering itself as a distinction within a universe of which it knows almost nothing except its primal, genetical skills of navigation making it environmentally aware, yet mindfully unaware of the eons of time still to come to test its qualities and meanings just as it has for expired eons of the past.

Normal is the alleged real world, the world of nature shaped by a celestial realization beyond the scope of any one species, cognizance, solution or belief as proof; rather than as the singled, attentive focus of an omnipotence, as if the infinite cosmos were simply the meager summed likeness of a shining, gilded light casting downward as a spotlight on one planetary stage.

Species would recklessly and futilely attempt to reach a captured environmental world of niche successes such as on this planet without this malleable spectrum of depthless equilibrium binding species together as a normalcy of biological, physical and chemical reality: explicitly culminating in the relatively recent past, arguably peaking at the beginning of its regression from fitful successes with the advent of humanity a mere tens or hundreds of thousands of years ago as a newfound, unleashed, fleeting ambition upon the lush natural world, consented by nature's obvious lack of impressive resistance.

Envisioning a Surreal World

Observing the succeeding system of a normal world practiced within the ecological circle proven by nature provokes a new enquiry: what, if anything, as a state within a collectively aware conviction, is surreality? As a concept, it is perceptual abstraction of reality as it exists in a current and past state, not much separated from hallucinations; or the upsurge of the unnatural and the embracing of manifold aftermaths within the complexity of reality's strangely unifying alternatives. It is an evolutionary shift from that which was proven over spanning epochs of millennia and contested through comparatively short generations by a defiant, asserting and ambitious progeny.

In this plausible surreality, interconnecting minds not only envision, predict and construct niche fulfillments as the opportunistic boons of genetic successes, but prove a world beyond an originating niche comprehension or intention of design. The surreal is the world of emotive environmental connectedness into fantastic, magnificent ideas contorting natural awarenesses, of proud, collected survival transformed into an imitating individuality of worded honors, as the obligation of illusive denials and odd beliefs as enlightenment, and as the malleability of emotive attunement into a plausible, complexing origin within humankind as the solely represented, uncontested challenger within the universe. The necessitated condition of surrendered instinctive and heroic belief into the appeasing explanation of mortality for impetus of action is the bewailing surreality of a newly raised, political world.

Surrealism is the unreasonable idea of meaning thrust upon humanity from nowhere except the exit from the jungle of life and embryonic reality, with the caressed, concocted idea of each subsequent generation holding to the belief of the exodus as completed, its status properly translated, and the distortion of this apparent meaning with and from its worldly origin as a privileged, just truth to be found and lived by for the furthering of human pride and its predictable, impending radiance upon either this world or the otherworld.

The old skills of nature are reshaped, retooled, and relentlessly readapted with unacknowledged primary aftershocks to the minds and bodies of human and nonhuman environments. This new skillset includes a vast range of unpausing past and occurred extinctions passing over as normal and without pangs of regret or the much-sought integrity of real, valued importance once extinct from the sketched memories of human observations.

Humanity enters a new, surreal world of its own founded atop the old reality much as life overcame the prior barren, inhospitable landscape of the early planet with the same imbalances of vigor.

In observing humanity's surreality, it can be contemplated what is normal in a world modeled by averages and majorities as guiding principles, by unfounded opinions and quirky moralities, and where truths are speculative prisms for the success and ruse of ambidextrous desires. Normal as a fully existing average or point could only occur in an unchanging, unevolved environment, one either never begun or fully concluded without potential for a further inserting solution to disturb the system into an abstract, abnormal state of discontinued deregulation.

This sense of normalcy is the spontaneous world of human surreality, much like the first peripheral absorption of environment by life inevitably consuming a planet in its diversity and shared diffusion spread by the branches of evolution with long-lasting generational space to cling to for support like an archive of solutions.

This method of forgiving an old world could alternatively be applied to growths of species and transitional solutions as native predictions of reality and the regulated variations of generational qualities, much like the essential range and advanced scope of diverse and convergent trait development in conjunction with niche environments, without one niche or species being the epitome of normal or origin, but of mutual forces embedded within the framework of life as a fountainhead of mutually attained actuality.

The is no energy or might in isolation, starved by a barren, dissipated reality erased of solutions and predations through the absence of environmental stimuli or the degradation of a supportive landscape for life other than humanity to attach.

The world of surreality is a world in which its wide absurdity is noisily pronounced but mostly unobserved and unfelt, and where the natural repercussions of such choices are normalized into appropriate behaviors through prefabricated, integrated systems of belief as ready choice for newly arriving participants to learn and succumb to admit as if without opportunity or alternative to its surrendered, closed state.

~~

It is difficult to define intention, an essential property to be skilled to correctly discern for better survival in the natural world, and how it is sourced as cause for action within a surreal world. Inclusive of the revilement readily permittable to nature as a lower rank, the ongoing successful dissociation must be learned within a same species by biased division mimicking nature's systems of change-encouraging, contending predations.

Individuality within the world increases and shifts from clans as knowledge and experience grows in associating specifics of environments to predicating memories and the roots of active opinions. When the world integrates newly discovered inspirations and individual-based inclinations into the traditional intentions of clan-based drives and the intermixing of a diversity of group-founded beliefs of the same environment as an inevitable outcome of growth, conscious knowledge of truths become broadly conflicted by the originating environment of a solitary planet within a vast universe of immediate, original ignorance as knowledge first begins to develop and gain symbolic retention to solid bits of cultivated information.

The improvement of retained conscious information for an uninhibited species, or the long retreat from an original illiteracy as predetermined by the fact of having an origin from which knowledge must begin, is not equally spanned or far removed across all individuals of all temporal states ranging an immensely affecting and overlooked current, prolonged moment of the surreal world.

The advent of original ignorance and its impending, evolving errors upon a calculating consciousness cannot be understated as an influence upon its proceeding comprehension of knowledge, no differently than its ageless pursuits of instinctual values during an original, niche-fathoming environmental world allegedly disclosed merely for consumption as the inevitable stepping stones provisioning the glutenous path to humanity's enormity.

Lacking through much of the history of this accumulation of environmental information over sequential epochs is the differing degrees of misunderstanding and disinformation, the entire spectrum of evidence as it exists to misleadingly confuse reciprocal to how it enlightens. As difficult as it is for conscious minds to find association with the obvious, realistic side of information, it is exceedingly more difficult finding the sources of disinformation's unsuspecting deficiencies outside the awareness of current visions of understanding. This arises due to a practical ineptitude in knowing what is further absent from satisfied conceptions, targeted opinions, and the scheming resourcefulness of predictability in its association with information previously wrought from reality into new contexts of eventful coordination.

This dichotomy of confidence is like being aware of a universal world through the inbred lens of surreal networks of acceptability alone, and the lost fondness for the natural world long considered offensive as fitting source of true empathy, or as further deliberation of spiritual meaning beyond incidental fodder for human physiological and ascending sustenance. The natural world is nonconsensual in its symbolic uses as essential, usurped betterment of solutions for humanity's inevitable consummating ascension as the winning, inimitable personification of everything a planet has to offer it.

In a current state of humanity, it can be hard to appreciate the power of original ignorance, even affronted by its thriving durability as it presently exists, upon the unawareness and inexperience of a budding, virgin consciousness as it first explored and began to find the wellspring of environmental knowledge, as the derivation of correlating symbols, as a beginning, empty of anything which exposes itself as closely reckoning it's meandering paths from instinctual experiences to the knotted strings of surreal learning.

With a suddenness transpiring over millennia, the human being is abruptly stated and duly recorded as highly conscious, self-aware and privileged by its starting witlessness, accepting the repercussions of all the emergent scenarios it will inevitably confusedly exude as a symbolized, surreal history of humanity indelibly written into the fabric of reality through its normalized acceptances among winning patterns of flouting: dissociating itself cleanly from the prior integrity of the world.

A private, imaginable world is suddenly possible where it never much existed before. There is a valid absence of culpability before fresh truths supplanting old ones, with its methods of measuring personal space and alleged freedoms of private awareness in the company of strangers all capable and deriving the same mixed, befitting and regulated ends. This privacy does not even have to exist in isolation but can be shared in associating experience by others just as eager to articulate and overcome its dizzying opportunities, to reveal its physical and mystically held promises, and to divulge its latent, appeasing realities to one another in celebratory ritual.

Life on a planet in this instance becomes a game for the world of humanity, a stratagem of *us against them* and *me against you*, even if some strategies seek transient cooperation or submission for its better survival in the precarious and consequential moments of long eons of history behaving much the same in innumerable, differing localized, overlapping and convergent contexts of history.

In cases, relative temporary isolation can promote values incapable of a jointly shared world due to the absence of palpable measures of risk as an outcome of its restricted approachability protecting against conflicting opportunities for elimination, creating a perilous future due the unwitting fact there is no lasting isolation cast as eternal success within the structured designs of its world.

The same could be stated for a species isolated within an unapproachable universe and its conceivable capacity to share a singular world bordered by cultures, shared as the mutual venerability of all species alongside nature as a hailed unifying journey, with each burdened by redundant perils to outwit.

The branching future outcomes of any challenge upon the dominance of an otherwise conceivably impossible fact of appearing clung atop a rotating, curved surface might appear endlessly unfathomable, other than for humankind making of it a perfect refuge for the newly discovered identity of an individuated self to generationally advance in play into an unsolicited, groping and sole choice of evolution for new participants to unquestionably follow without alternative.

This contest within reality for supremacy translates into an exclusion from the preceding, cosmic world as souled substantiality to a purported, inner, human-specified world. The new unseen world is discovered to afford an efficient motivation for encouragement against the nonresponsive celestial backdrop exposed through nature's inability to properly defend itself against its mistaken, losing roll of the dice. By its proper actions, humanity is absolved of its effects by the rightful cause of its surreal rewards.

~~

Among the synchronized contributors growing a viable species over millennia, a real world can appear vastly different simply due to standpoint, the delicate traits and cultures of followers, and the idiosyncrasies of the manifold environments it arises into as an influence upon its willing capacity to act as identified entities. Within the scattered realms throughout history, humanized niches were found, wrought and defended no different than the rest of nature and its niche-satisfying, conjoined environmental medleys of self-wreaking genera, as species have recurred its defense for a relative eternity of years.

Something observable in one mind is unobservable in another simply due to a differing sensitivity of indications willfully associating the makings of reality, due to subtleties of variation among members' shared genetic construct, pragmatic natural encounters, localized reoccurring traits of species and eccentric mysticism.

These variations are natural and could be considered normal for such a species as its means of surviving diverse external risks towards advancing solutions while still supporting the signatory identity of the species as a collective. Some of these variations involve differing patterns of perception, making entire collections of individuals of a species capable or incapable of manifold posturing of mind and control of body within reality based on genetic prevalence within the whole by its inheritable proportionality and cultured emergence into reality.

A suddenness of appearance should be a consideration of human resolve: as if we don't realize as a species the abruptness of our newly conscious arrival within reality and its contended meanings.

There are deliberately misguiding perceptive beliefs of this emergence as a surfacing of the human-made universe: needed to exist as a workable, long-standing solution for surreality to best persevere in the tendencies of humanity's future meanings.

Expectations of authentic outcomes when dealing with the attached opinions of commingling groups of individuals within a surreal, concocted world is an expectation to be overcome and purposely inhibited within the vulnerable mind composed of aspergic believability. Within crowds, there is a seeking dispassion as a best means of protecting an essential impassioned identity as a nostalgia for the motives compelling undeterred individuality.

The crowd exposes denied, misleading talents within the complex routines of societal enactivism. The aspergic personality can become absorbed in distraction, lost in self-engagement within a crowd of reaching ideas and the promoted insertions of wildly divergent, motivated, influential exchanges of experience and ideas of truth. Truth loses its aura of authenticity as it becomes a benefit unique to individuals while dynamically grouped to localized cultured opinions and forceful, exaggerated credence.

~~

Aspergic tendencies can establish a lifelong process of rebellious, reciprocated self-learning and self-teaching, whether the lessons taught are from oneself or insightful others during watchful experiences seeking new, keen-sighted inspirations to be marked by patterned, humorously strange and unexpectedly connected presences. It makes an individual believe in a perceived world which exists better in the enactions of others, while the real world of behaving, sensing and seeing a differently textured reality becomes an alleged fantasy.

These fantastic awarenesses dimly meld into a world of alleviating entertainment and the organized consumption of instinctive essence into a differently coiled identity in its association with absolving the excruciating stamina of time. This detachment is learned through experiences of long lingering deliberation usually to utter exclusion as a persuasive factor on selection within the realm of human surreality to which it is not precisely related primarily due to its fitness being deemed as inappropriateness, untranslatable, or not of a proper kind.

Confronted by resistance and a sense of defeating self-doubt at an overwhelming, isolating mainstream, distrust inevitably will affect decisions, in oneself and in relationships with others due to personal inhibitions mesmerizing the normal spheres of popular plausibility.

Doubt emerges from the sense of being so minimal in relevance that one solitary viewpoint must be benign in context with such celebrated popularity, especially without the resolve to observe with appreciation divergent experiences of mind and body in conjunction with the stimulus of accepting the preestablished, affecting worldly environment. This current environment is collected and endured over eons, purposely structured into the proffered reality as the one to be welcomed into by an unsolicited rite of individual birth among its recurring lines of unproven, alternative successes, organized to warmly embrace its first and subsequent moments.

Overcoming the world enough to embrace this resistance can produce great benefits, reciprocally for the individual and the humanity it might immeasurably inspire. Subjugation to this resistance can create a disheveled, conflicted and soothing solution for the aspergic individual, and a comfort for others to dismiss as a better fitting representation of how a shockless, mystifying normalcy is supposed to be carefully imitated.

Normalcy comes to be a loss of control to be expectantly found yet not to be fully acted upon to avoid hardening a lasting replica of identity. For the aspergic attention, resistance itself becomes a means of control, not as a stepping above others, or as judgement necessarily directed at other standpoints, but as a simple method of finding support in oneself without loss of identified difference. This sense of identity is compromised by repeating reoccurrences of reality exhibited through the seepage of emotions conjoined with perceptively sensual sensitivities exuded during human interactions impossible for an aspergic awareness to ignore without simply not looking or not giving direct attention to it as a method of distraction, and with a confident persistence much like pride.

Aspergic attitudes perceive the surreal world like a fusion of past and present, a happening of temporal disassociations difficult at times to detect with a sustained willpower to watch its reoccurred histories. They must recognize to contend with the fact they contain at least some measure of the assumed absence within allistic observations when it comes to accepting believable foresight, much like an equalizing constant of mathematics necessitated by the origin of personality and its requested validations of appeasement at an expectable social product.

In the observances of neurotypical adoptions, this subjugation eventually comes to be a directed expectation furthering the overwhelming opinion of normalcy. Normalcy becomes repelled by natural societal resistances. These repellant reactions are often not much separate from fears of unawareness, of what is unknown through allistic experiences and its envisioned ownership of the world's physical bigger picture without the loaded subtlety of exhaustive undertones.

To an aspergic personality, allistic normalcy can be an enthrallment contrary to a naturally minded quest for equilibrium as a relationship with all reality. There can be guilt over one's own social inadequacy. Inane separation can come from not wanting to impose such great exertion requirements on most others for the sake of a singular attending identity.

There are many real capacities of furtherance the world does not observe except through the focusing lens of aspergic and other non-allistic perceptions, including the deprivations of nonhuman and human sensitivities as premeditation; at times, only later in life do these self-requesting personalities become alert to vital adaptations to allistic facets within the everyday world of normalized surreality through a discreet, nondisclosed relationship of endurable unification with it as an evolved, private adaptation.

Aspergic personalities persuasively learn they must adapt to whatever others resemble as personality, intention of opinion and willingness of action for a vaster collective popularity, but struggle with the implications of approaching evidences observed to be naturally worse on the integrity of the world than to adapt not as a mimicking of others as sameness but as an imitating likeness attempting to preserve a minimalized involvement, and thereby a less convincing temptation.

This is not easy as a choice for an aspergic attention to accept as the condition of socialized identity within the realm of humanity due its overall lack of prior and current credibility given by its many generational shortcomings. There is palpable evidence of its believable erosion of attention realized within the observable world of practiced humanity not realized within the observable universe or the innovations of nature as elucidation.

Allistic minds will often assume a required, intimidating adjustment due a strange personality being isolated and labelled, as an imposing, expected requirement from that other, observably unresponsive, intimidating persona to clearly sense. It is self-appeasement, and an unwillingness to learn and adapt oneself, which strongly motivates the neurotypical mind full of its own vast assortments of motivated behaviorisms more damaging in scale and likelihood of experience within the world, all considered collectively acceptable as recognized talents of what properly defines normalcy of active attentions, however limited or overcompensated in scope of imagination, imitating talents and the command of personality in calibrating context while riding the unfettering waves of surreality.

~~

Often, though scarcely recognized without prewarning, an aspergic person can be a circumstance of enaction for allistic individuals not otherwise found in the experiences of everyday affiliation among a mainstream of duplicating individualities, encountered as a selective opportunity for openness or suspicion as an austere persona, to uncover a seeming eccentricity as either interesting or as a personal affront to the well-worn uses of traditional acceptability.

These sporadic opportunities will not be equal in outcomes, mainly due to the mutuality of the tangled, preestablished dissimilarity in allistic perceptions instead commonly and misguidedly interpreting the aspergic personality to be a haughty exaggeration of normalcy or simply too challenging a discrepancy in perceptual readability beyond the urgent spectrum of allistic normalcy to believe; or unvalued of further chasing for its unique resolve. This disinterest can reinforce an emotive separation experienced by the aspergic mindset, further enabling the recessed appreciation of social dissociation and the internal depths of a marked, isolated identity.

Aspergians observe the paths of balance within the environment of existence as an irresistible desirability, enthralled by the detailed implications of an unconflicted, genderless nature and an existence demonstrating an introverted caution, a simple complexity and an unwavering, embracing confidence in wide-ranging transformations being inherent as a movement to the structured frolic of reality.

During social interactions with and observable between people, it is the recognition of one or an assortment of idiocentric traits observed, preserved and re-sought as pleasing repetition or rediscovery, of related preceding moments occurring as a future memory finding entangled context during the happenstances of the rolling present experience.

The aspergic belief can be one of an acute relationship with reexperiences during the occurrences of current experiences.

The aspergic identity pursues the gifted sensations of a bodily mind, aiming to substitute for the same or better perceptions as any other unbiased person, mutually assigned and existing as a mere potential connection within the happenings and the dynamics of the unavoidable human encounter with its own species during a lifetime within the pre-created world.

This makes surreality for the aspergic inquisitiveness an intended, alternative world in its usual absence of stimulus other than, at best, unattainable idyllic or idolized inklings of normalized, mystical unreality as the inspiring fodder for reaching remotely comprehendible human spiritual realms.

~~

There is overabundant exertion attached with retaining the past as an inner working mechanism of connotations, a playing field of self-analysis, rather than a dismissively selective approach to the retention of personal memory in its association with the world, as external identification within societal milieus and its cues for an identifying personality to be proudly donned.

The demands of memory retained as strict replication can be confounding to an aspergic perception, especially without the direct appreciation reciprocally gained and lost through a normalizing genetic diagnosis or causal behavior patterns as familiar clarification which would have been prevalent until the recent past: whereby aspergic individuals lived without knowledge of a difference in their perceptive insights, assuming the distinction an error of processing against a vast array of contrary personalities. In another context, it saved these individuals the victimizing shame of being labelled as exceedingly broken rather than simply overlooked, if not wrecked on exhibition in a personalized asylum. Thereby reality creates, through constriction of alternative identity customized as forceful conformity to escape, convincingly self-identified persons in contrary belief of a personal normalcy.

With the requirement of memory retention as a method of associating past, present and probable futures, there is aspergic difficulty in letting go of the billowing meld of personally salient past events as pointed markers for later structured use. The aspergic personality can come to cravenly seek newer experiences for improved associations of reality as it is properly actualized.

This occurs without much recourse however alienly conflicted an individual aspergic persona might be in comparison within their own emotively thought experiences as they try to grasp the eccentric world they find themselves exposed to while juxtaposed with a composition of motivating, externally composed worldly intentions beyond much aspergic interest or true reassurance as ownership.

Non-aspergic persons, by their own sketches of normalcy, are different through allistic tendencies while existing in commonality. The aspergic person exists within separate parameters of perceptions and feelings of thought in response, often without realizing until later the parameters are different, while finding common imitation within the surfacing landscapes of existence, creating an internal person in conflict with its own human-made environments inclusive of massed, perpetrating identities: unless exiled to an intimately sought refuge of private self-making.

This straying departure allows for new insights and abstract approaches due to a demanded ability to view the world in other plain dimensions of evidence outside the bounds of allistic human normalcy.

The retention of strict memories also applies to human histories, where the past is not easily or even possibly overlooked as a source for higher truths, repeating patterns of behaviors as explanations for the past and current state of humanity within the world, with the passion of a nourishing elucidation others do not necessarily know the compulsion to seek and the confidence to admit.

In social interactions, an aspergic-leaning personality can become possessed of an imbalance in responses due to a retained relationship with happenings through heightened memory and the reexperiencing, newly associating sensitivity to the impulses of memory during the moments of occurring encounters: more as a convincing fondness for focused dissociation than a disordered conduct. This experience can be heightening when experienced in conducive isolation, surrounded by preferred events, or likable settings and gatherings.

Aspergic tendencies creates an observer, a seeker of occasions for latent delving without having to be a direct participant. The aspergic person becomes the cause for the effect on normalcy and the mainstream it is imposed upon as an odd, discomforting suspect. If the two interject calmly there is some measure of sensitive phases of normalcy within the array of personalities making up this state of unfinished experiences. An aspergic identity will correlate experienced attributes of the temporal and spacial world not looked for or suspected by the normalized world of fixed, believable harmonies.

Reality is a lure, its textured, thinly coated truths readily plain to accept in an aspergic personality must be arduously striven to acceptance in the normalized mind excessively devoid of aspergic tendencies as a clear, gifted abnormality.

~~

Aspergic belief is unfettered trust in its recognition of a post-truth and post-ethical world traversing the depths of events and experiences back to a near origin, while questioning the validity of the prefix "post-" throughout human history as a context. It appears more as a constancy or more proper to the prefix "pseudo-" or "anti-" in its relationship with the evolution of humanity's collectively aware acceptance of allistic identity within its reworked surreality. It is a lack and confusion of human history which transcribes the prefix "post-" to something which appears new but is truly ancient and likely has always been since a far distant infancy of conscious belief in its own tarnished, transcribed supremacy.

An aspergic person can come to empathize with nature as an association of marked context and reverence in status associated to a contrasted dominance of otherwise allistic overbalance among humankind.

~~

Though enjoying the strategy and thrill of games, Aspergians might not like to take part in real world gameplay unless truly called due to appropriate fitting cause of challenge. This cause, it is learned through experience, is prevalent in the actual surreal world of humanity. Games can permit the aspergic mindset insight into normalized strategies, useful as a means of identifying it better within the real world during the interactions with others, or as better recognition of injustice, harm, and manipulation in the motives of other persons assumed differently contended.

An aspergic person can be intensely skilled to perform and maneuver in such a world, but lacks the motive of the rewards, or prefers different rewards for inspiration elsewhere, even if not readily apparent, as an unsought challenge confidently trailed and trusted in uncertainty. In cases, it can manifest in remuneration to those deserving with the prior confidence of will and current motivation to play such strategies in the world against its own species and all other species as if an indifferently rationalized pride above the mainstream in the context of allegedly undeniable successes.

~~

Recognition can end opportunity for growth in defining ongoing beliefs and the emergent intuitiveness which surfaces from its wellspring of insights. The perceptions of others knowing a difference will shape the occurrences of identity which determine the aspergic individually not much differently than any other is shaped by environmental influence, except in the scope of its intense presence between individuality and surreality as contradiction.

Often, aspergic perceptions will find patterns within reality which the conscious mind will not become aware of until later under pertinent circumstances with a sense of being found while having been unconsciously initiated somewhere before in the environment, usually with remembrance as if a sense of familiar reoccurrence. The experience can be thought of as how a gene might appear benignly at one time, only to find essential use in regulating later gene patterns into a new solution otherwise unworkable without the earlier, previously inert gene being already present. A similar description could be made for viewed fundamental particles of physics as an evolvement of solutions.

~~

Aspergic tendencies could be a genetically regulated advancement; or an attempt at finding a path back from a normalized surreal world to a renewing association with a natural world; or a regressive deregulation for what is no longer required within a niche interpretation originally instilled by nature.

Aspergic talents recognize the spirituality in solutions of nature much as shamanism of ancient wanderers. Either is of equal value and difficulty whether perceived with a resolved, leaning preference towards real or surreal physical mysticism. For the betterment of the species in past environments, not all individuals are equally physical or mystical in their attentiveness except through the long-stringed attachment of forgotten origins.

Certainly, there are environments where the physical world reigns supreme over an absently perceived mysticism as an unchosen state, just as there are affordances for mystically bent individuals matched to sacredly insightful environments as dynamic enlightenment, as a type of idealized attunement of bodily survivability.

The spiritual experience can be of greater or lesser value than the physical one, yet over the range of its time-based totality usually assumes completed, poised equilibrium: even if not fully stable within any one of countless individuals during any one of endless observed moments of specific time and space.

~~

A lack of allistic admittance of a spectrum of differing empathies is an aspergic difficulty to contend; an obstructive self-admittance of the shiftiness of beliefs without counter awarenesses made through personal identifications of reality. It is difficult to admit of oneself what others cannot observe without the direct prejudice of prior knowledge; it's not as easy to guess at as it is to be suspicious of as an expected mode of allistic response to the nonexistent, unsuspecting unknown in all its vigor and telling scents.

Aspergic tendencies create a contrast which promotes conflicted responses of emotive discernment towards reality, increasing the probability of a revolting, contemplative, torn and dynamic personality mostly unobservable through normal, expected depictions of others except given the accusations against their actions.

Recognition that intuition can be fooled as easily as ideas can coerce a mind to act due to the inherent, malleable exertion required in balancing mutual understanding. Words can be difficult to use as an implement for explaining ideas, since the interpretations available for other minds due the use of words can often create confusions of perspective according to divergent past intentions, experiences and pent resentments.

With aspergic tendencies advanced within an individual, guessing is especially difficult yet still essential to social interactions. It is all guesswork against expected intentions as a predictability of ongoing experiences, and the dispiriting conflict of inconsistency between a singular identity and a disparaging, constricting mainstream.

As an avoidance of rudeness, an aspergic personality does not initially or boldly offer to others what should be predicted in return as an invitation to brave rewards of exchange.

~~

There is an urgently growing passion to recognize identity in the environment, but aspergic influence is short in the world as revealed by aging readings of past and current human history where the aspergic personality cannot find proper connection with its proportionally integrated nonappearance within human society.

Strangely, as a method of deflecting simple, subtle dishonesty, an adversely normalized allistic value, there is aspergic comfort in being unobserved, in being without expressive opinions even as imitation of integration within plainly sighted multitudes of concentrated sentiments and interpretations, and the desire to further its sating lack of detection as an involvement with such whirlwinds of compulsory, socializing anarchy.

A nurtured reaction can arise from the obligation to not reveal the discomfiture of identification to others as an inevitable stone to carry, and as it is destined to reoccur in a normalized world minimally persuaded by aspergic urgings of betterment.

~~

Avoidance is a need for trust and certitude not found in the current environment, but in the environment of identity instead as a sanctuary. Words, actions and emotional arousals which express such certitude are sought out with greater trust, salient against a backdrop of empty actions, polished words and the presumptions of self-aroused excitements.

Possessed of personas which are not so much viewable from the outside as they are experienced as a secret privilege is a splitting, uneasy state to dwell within, especially when contextualized within a reality normalized by contrary states of mindsets perilous in beliefs and actions, making of reality a seemingly more dangerous place to exist, far beyond the immediate risks of survival once bound to the natural world for sustenance, the attunement of skilled traits within tightened groups and inspired, instinctive individuality. For the aspergic persona, surreality can appear to be a tightened constriction suffocating the natural integrity of instinctive values.

Distancing from others can be a sympathetic reaction symptomatic of aspergic empathy, one of overall wonder at the emotions of existence primally shadowing the mutual affectations of humanity as an endeavoring, forgotten rapport.

Often, there is resistance is saying what should be said, acting upon what action should be taken, or is calculated should be said or done due to inadequate personal evidence and the preestablished predictions surfacing from haunting past experiences.

This resistance is too unreceptive and avoidable within the chaotic external world, forcing the inevitable result of needing to quietly watch what is being missed in surreality with its confusing motives of thought and intending beliefs of reality once easily fathomed as a naturally motivated predestination favoring humanity. Often what is being overlooked is done with a profoundly aware purpose intensely safeguarded and usually unhindered by implications.

Individuals can be constrained to look further forward instead of simply backward in seeking a practiced anticipation of an eventual emotive destiny: through other means of strategy beyond the normalized, shortened immediacy of a human edifice as it exists to an aspergic perspective as a context for needing a more genuine closeness of experience with reality, as an involved participant and attempt at coinciding experiences without the challenge of a human-instilled handicap. The aspergic mindset must also contend with the delicate association of experience to resistance, and the loss of rewarding benefits should its peculiar hiddenness be diluted by exposure to the blending nature of a unifying, surreal acceptance.

Aspergic tendencies lean toward suppressed detection of the accurately divulged realities and integrities of identity, contended against the allistic credentials of humanity as a species in context with nature and reality in its incompleteness and brittle durability. Such tendencies conflict with humanity's surreal creation of itself as a cresting epitome of physical and spiritual dominance.

Such cognizance describes a depth of what is viewed in deliberated experiences through the assuming aptitudes of one species within an otherwise impossible reality. Perception becomes communally shared to omit the burdened delay of deliberation, through calculating attempts at associative insights through the shiftability of the everchanging world, with attention for the consequences of the unfathomable as a realizable embryo, while possessed of an attentive, emotively introspective relationship with experience, not just humanity, nature or nonhumanity but the wholeness of reality as if existing long before the urgent need for the prerequisite of personalized identity.

There is aspergic acknowledgement such poise should be naturally endowed and easily uncovered through a confident belief in personal action performed in attuned conjunction with a realized existence without alternative or the asking for more beyond simple betterment of survival, and a niche acceptance of equalized mind, body and environment bonded to the universal forces buttressing its successes.

~~

Aspergic mindsets may tend to systematize reality's dependable associations, including emotive, social and identity realizations. It becomes easier to systemize the facets of reality than the duplicitous performances of humanity broadly prevalent and beyond true self-conceptions, which creates an anonymity in dealing with the world which disobeys confidence, and thereby reciprocally blunting or enhancing chosen actions. Sometimes this multidirectional maneuvering is lost to chance through the simple temporal expenditure of calculating the vigor and evidence vital in having conviction during personal choices, and the requirement of correctly deciding action and inaction without slothful obesity in justifying convictions.

As an unnatural presence within the crowd, Aspergians must assume the disguises of surreality without wanting to appear disguised. The natural world does not fit as a costume any longer to humanity in its current state of bodily social evolution, making vastly ranged populations strangers to the natural world of their own origin and birthright, and the many instincts and associations of passions gifted as an actuality for the confines of a species within a created, shapely environment, and within an individual of a species fluidly awed within themselves at the candor of a naturally occurred existence and an alleged fitful place within it.

Aspergic tendencies can be considered a natural construct for the potential of nature's self-adoration through the absorption of such a reflective presence in a perceptually blank, felt stare, like a mirror for reality's pride.

Aspergians prefer to become emotively attached to this mutual intention between reality and the experience of perceptions, as a bodily and mindful representation of this mutual incredibleness, as a living texture and coalescing exhibition of a recollected hiddenness of reality and the evoked power of silence. Minimally recognized among multitudes, aspergic seeking finds agreement with this hidden silence as a shared memory of worldly success and a whispering empathy floating the waves of reality.

Sadly counter-intuitive, a proportionality of aspergic persons are bound to become lost in the complexities of a surreal world and later defiantly averse to the hints of the natural world as an ill-fated outcome.

~~

Imitating has a successful prevalence in nature and societal expectations of real and surreal normalcy, from disguises of body and mind, concealments of milieus, the estrangements of natural environments and redirected bodily stimuli into believable actions and responses, and as defenses against behavioral intentions due the intrusiveness of the world beyond each individual by whatever shaped design. It isn't a solely human phenomenon, though humankind has widely assumed its pride. It is not owned as a familiarity except as a characteristic of satiating a niche outcome within a natural world.

Even in the absence of mirroring, there is recognition of imitation in others and recognition of its seeming absence in oneself. As well, there can be a detection in other persons of a nonmirrored rejection of this absence or particular non-attempt at an expected simulated response: conflicting no different than its absence is solely recognized as an absence without much appreciated attention to the mimicking of purposeful normalized expectancy as a strange, surreal obligation.

This mirroring, conceived as a trait of survival, has its own budding advantages stemming from its accepted recognition as a trait through the intentioned compulsions of benefit within the imposing compositions of everyday life.

With aspergic inclinations, an individual is self-observed not mirroring alongside others through the subtle, postured reactions of comforted reply, but as witness within a personal, aspergic context of the absence of the trait not observed in reply as expectations within neurotypical minds driven by the reassuring predictability of acceptably configured, genetically regulated social echoing.

While perceiving Aspergians, allistic perspectives can be conflicted as they try to naturally imitate a trait which is non-expressed or differently expressed within the normalized individuals due the confounded absence of pleasing rewards motivating properly satiated anticipations or, more appropriately, a red flag to its affronted expectedness within an immediate environment epitomized by a challenging, unfixed aspergic presence.

These conformities to convicted expectations in social behaviors are the appeasement of inconsistent integrities resulting from each individual's capacity to predict the repetitive world with differing experiential capacities, understandings and skills in ongoing optimism of correct responses from a preferably nonconflicted but often conflicted world in its relationship to the experiences of a defined personality and any attempt at embracing a retained identity.

Aspergic tendencies can be an affront to these reward-seeking expectations and the comforting grounding it supplies as mutual reexperience of pleasing reassurances within a social playground. Obviously, rarer individuals not perceptually comforted in equal measure by the same rewards of social anticipation through imitation, seeking and finding alternate means of self-approval with the world, will be exceptionally observed and naturally suspect of questionable, even disloyal rebelliousness as an opinion of an appeasement-seeking allistic attention.

These attempts at mirroring can seem more as a struggling type of mocking rather than as imitating from the aspergic-inclined perspective, as a feature to learn to acceptingly understand even at the exclusion of oneself from the equation if that is the highest probability of overall success in retaining a sought neutrality.

No different than the mimicking of the mirror impulse achieved in mutuality as reciprocal recompence is prevalent in a normalized social world, it will find resistance as an attempt at exchange in an aspergic-minded personality, forcing an unexpected disagreement with surreal normalcy against such a determination to observably outwill it in its supposed act of contempt to decorum; rather than continue accepting and acting upon the original, disagreeing impulse not found profoundly existing other than rigidly within the habituated expectancy of neurotypical minds and their alleged preordained world of erected, idolized creation perfectly customized for proven human mechanization.

A neurotypical mind trying to mimic an aspergic mind through accidental environmental interactions can have difficulty with its legibility. This recognition can be bluntly affronting and re-represented in return creating unnatural reactions enabling the higher prospects for conflicts resulting from the allistic mindset's inability to recognize the aspergic mind as something contrarily distinct, much as nonhumanity is not considered distinct in its highly unifying awarenesses absent through the latency of nature's undertone.

The aspergic presence must learn to contend with an overwhelming external difference while the neurotypical mindsets can often live entire lifetimes without a desire to experience or believe in this difference allegedly fathomed by others as if a mystical disbelief in reflective physicality like an illusory manipulation of light.

This relationship can be a potentially profitable pursuit of associative learning and sympathetic understanding due the necessity of utilizing perceptual aspergic skills over the same lifetime as a stimulating, unceasing resolve fixed within an otherwise conflicting reality in need of successfully being contended as a normalcy of survival.

This necessitated analysis of the environment for cues and information can be an added benefit for a proficient, aspergic mind in need of better connotations in understanding contrary normalized, neurotypical beliefs of reality as an overwhelming inequality.

Each identity is mutually unchained in spirited bias of sensual withdrawal, in their confused inhibitions in reading another identity and the believability of opinions over observations. As an opportunity of unification, the coexistent aspergic and neurotypical natures can also mutually empathize, even if this empathy is solely encountered through amiable understandings among less counted individuals: gained through the shared associations rewarded by a close commonness of afforded experiences unified through a coincidentally bonding spiritual, emotive or believable motivation.

Aspergic pride inevitably needs to win out at whatever costs or resulting gains are craved to occur as reparation. Aspergic tendencies force an individual to try actions meant to socialize and to do unnaturally what a vast mainstream of neurotypical dispositions find natural, with reassuring consent and adept skills required of its vibrant social arena exhausting the dominating surreal world.

This breach of opposing ownerships enhances the difficulty of self-enabled aspergic gauging of predictable scenarios of actions expected of its world, as if a non-actress among actors, often misconstrued through social normalizations as timidity, introversion, or vague frailty of character spooked by an obvious allistic detection of internalization cast from the aspergic persona.

Through a lacking of perceptive aptitude within many neurotypical sensitivities prevalent within aspergic aspirations of reality as a different kind of unhindered normalcy, there is a mutual mistrust of intention due to differing perceptions not needing to find acceptance within the neurotypical mind as readily as it does within the aspergic mind as compromise according to the natural imbalances of encouragement embodied within the allistic structures of surreality.

The disproportion is the evolutionary skirmish of biased corroboration within the world's designs. It is not just a lack of understanding but a lack of acceptance of what can be understood, and a lack of willingness to burden with the requested empathy for the deep implications of tolerating manifold versions of truths, compassions and sighted beliefs as a seeming unity of its spiritual perfection within the physical, environmental world of surreality in all its reoccurring outcomes.

This is meant to be circumvented as an unsuccessful path to be best avoided for the betterment not of humanity or most of its individuals but for the instillation of forces capable of furthering the capacities of the species persuaded by its surreal encouragement of reality to bitter ends.

The disharmony emerges within the purposes of direct and indirect communications and bodily relationships of posturing and counter-posturing, forcing an aspergic persona to learn to be consciously secretive of unconscious impulses happening within the environment, enchantments of what others really do not want to hear or observe as a likeness of truth contained within a solitary, staring observant presence withstanding crowded, sensory disquiet with a steadfast resolve not to cede a colored petal of self-possession.

~~

An aspergic person distinguishes between sincere and disingenuous in the flowing interpretations of experiences. This recognition can be observed within the most pertinent memories retained through an advancing lifetime for reflective prophecies of expectation such as should be predictable to neurotypical minds from the aspergic perspective; instead repeatedly observing an apparent lacking or absence of sightedness for such finely lighted spectacles.

Natural symbols of instruction are retained for future use from past practices, and the aspergic identity inevitably learns to apply likelihoods as a compensating solution to the necessity of social interactions, reckoning with performances, motives, intentions and risks as a persistent ritual of enabled allistic attention.

The aspergic person can come to overlook themselves in this perceptive game of educated guessing, whereby the world can seem to exist as something *including* them in relevance identical to a freeing, pressing sense of personal exclusion from it as an identified, fragmenting right of spacial independence.

~~

Aspergians tend to try to act on motivations not exactly for personal gain or redemption but for overall betterment beyond oneself as a whispered echo and tendrilled influence on future outcomes. Sometimes, this betterment of reality is not yet plain but merely a disenchanting envisioning or prophecy not readily sought or yet presented within a strangely surreal reality demanding reckless self-attentions of its individuals given to one convergently multi-devised interpretation.

This intended betterment can also be illusive and is prone to premeditated, divergently ill-fated penalties surfaced from the past as an endless, nourishing consummation within the present state of the world.

~~

There are private aftermaths embedded within individuals according to the benefitted extent of livingly robust, visual memories as a possession of mind continually seeing the colored details of a tidally conflicting surreality placed atop reality. These memories can be kept as an obligation of survival for the aspergic person incapable of merely generous recollection. Memories are retained according to the value to the one remembering, so that they become important or not based on the same implements of detection or imitation of the past in context to the memory's sole ownership within existence as a potential avenue for advantage by exploitation. Memories become means to an analysis of a personal history and its merits or basis of contention as an identity. Memories can also be altered to reflect a false sense of personal history and empowerment within a caricaturized, unproved or victimized individuality.

It is rare to find these distinctions found within the fabrics of surreality expressed by other personas; instead through the concentration produced by inspiring books, art, the looks of nature and the collected, reflective insights of experience within reality retained through discovered, inclusive events as living aspects of the past.

History as a probing feedback can become a fitting source of discovery, learning the exuded proclamations of similar confined, improperly fitted aspergic presences as they coped and summated a value to the reality they experienced during any of countless strange epochs of time, with the vigor of lifelong rebellious personas trying to find a face of identity within a spiritually misrepresented, shadowed atmosphere of conned worldly identity.

Aspergic minds can look to the past for source of solidarity, individual exertions of will and striving, enduring minds lived in unknowing contrast and without proper context within an ordinary, temporal world.

~~

There can exist a sense of solitary disassociation with the world of moveable occurrences around an aspergic perspective seeing not only the results of behaviors in the world but the impulses, motives, designs and insights of the alleged processes causing them. They feel and sense the inner workings of natural reality as betterment without the confidence of certitude in oneself as a fitting source due to minimalized encouragement from a preferably suspicious, contrarily perceptive world differently explained. This intuition needs to be tended through a lifetime of experience and self-reflection against and alongside the unseeing contrast of inversely disposed multitudes to be fully appreciated.

Due to the negligible inspiration of aspergic tendencies within surreality, the overwhelming cause of the disparity felt and sensed is a neurotically infused world of overconfident actions and unrepaired consequences without much genuine foresight, attention or predictability observable as inner workings of its world. Instead, it exists as a world prevailing without much sensitivity beyond or destined to the moment. As a context, it is visibly a disobedience to a previously teeming natural world and aged universe before the advent and tussle of personalities surfaced as a minor, misled contention of true proportional value, especially without proper measurement scaling a member of a species against an infinitely separated cosmos.

The world has amassed a multitude of intricate details with unsorted connections without any conceivable or realistic overall bigger picture. The big picture of humanity is one of perpetual conflict over rambled fantasies inside its secured, embracing surreality, a world constructed as guard against the overwhelming exposure of the universe upon all chosen, isolated actions in belief of its supremacy over a natural planet brimming with aged successes, against a natural world of private nonhumanity, against its own species and generational futures of offspring, and as reply to a cosmos quieted to its secret, permissive and satiating pleasures.

Focus and rightfully perceiving specific interests and observances of reality can act as a method for clearing the obscurity of many small details into something tangible and real, much like physical matter clings to the preestablished forces of an endless summated past for support and substantiality within the same universe, shortening its focus and permitting evolution as the spirited vigor of actuality in all its gained poise; beyond a shrunken consciousness limited in its ability to observe the world further than its abbreviated facts and definitions masking a self-reflecting schema of control.

~~

A residing spirit freed of the human-erected world to the extent of a journeying self-deniability contrary to its confidence, as a lively source of wonderment or insight for the identity of the individual, as something other than renunciation of the natural world in favor of imaginings of cosmic spiritual favoritism, is the tendencies of the aspergic-minded person in the pursuit of interpretations as a surfacing relationship with existence.

Aspergic tendencies must learn to deny presumed attentions and opinions of reality to enable private social influence upon emotive thinking to be the mere appeasing of mainstream expectancy. There can remain a lingering sense of doubt at the effectualness of these internalized denials as a self-corruption of skills at having to simply play along. It is most difficult when the aspergic person finds no joint support for its brand of interpretations within prevailing local and broader temporal environments.

In some cases, deniability of surreality can become widespread within the cognizance of an aspergic person, conflictedly learned as a confident self-fulfillment, the capacity to overlook oneself as an acting aspect of the coercive influences of a species, society and an environment lacking in true empathic explanations of the world, as an urgent, unappealing and unremitting craving for an enacted separateness from ownership.

An aspergic personality can be coerced by the prevalent conditions of a world to spend an entirety of a life taking on its inner makings, enduringly rebellious, thoughtful and silently inspired to transcend the contrariness of the surrounding reality perceived as textured differently than it is presented and believed through intimate experiences with normalized social adaptations.

Such minds must learn to understand when and when not to act on what can be at times an overvalued reading of individuated firsthand intentions and emotional states when merely occurring as an internalized awareness separate from the event, creating an individual who must control emotional impulses and mindful states internally envisioned without true ownership of all that the surreal incessantly represents as its objective manifestations of pursuit.

This creates a sensitively complex, withheld condition within an individual in relationship with the world, as empathic observations can lead to the sense of needing detachment from self-involvement due a neglected sympathy to what is beyond controlling, avoiding personal connections as beyond the scope of being an influential identity within the varied inactions, motives and designs of the human-made world, thereby adding another deep layer of separation within the aspergic person through self-designed relinquishment of ownership of the world, as if the world really did not belong equally to all in its representations of admittance.

The individual must extract these integrities solely through the experience itself as an acute alternative that is lived upon as discipline against the receiving of events otherwise deficient in mutual attainment.

Aspergic minds become an overcompensating origination of an extreme and risky environment beyond any conception of nature in relative scope. Without this condition of environmental influence assuming such a dominant comprehension of an otherwise unimaginable world, an aspergic mind, no different than the allistic mind, should evolve as a force within reality along separate and differing waves of represented, composed revelations.

Though, as recompense, with the current world existing in a current and past state of misinterpretation, the seeking aspergic identity finds as rewards its utmost talents, whereby reality itself becomes the artful canvas for the deft strokes and storming colors of emotive, mastered artists bursting with secret sightedness.

~~

It can at least be imagined the many individuals throughout human history until the most current present state with varied degrees of aspergic tendencies yet living without knowledge of a difference or even the notion of a differentiation existing as a possibility to be considered within human sensitivities and its eccentric new world of acceptable ideals: and the temporal fears associated with such bold revelations among ill-informed listeners. Of these individuals, there would be the likely few to succeed and the many to fail against the struggling pretense of a social persona contrary to an intuited nature: a subjected identity inside an objectified surreality while beyond a natural, justifiable context of support.

They have lived in a world while perceiving existence as surfaced differently and consistently without thinking it anything other than normal in the staring eyes of an inquisitive persona colored within the usual inattention of everything else in widespread black and white, surrendering to calls of victimizations, mental afflictions, tortures of forced concession as compromising penalty for any possessively raised awareness of social confidence.

In such a mindset, any idea of contradiction is overshadowed by the varying ideas of the spectrum of equality and misrepresentations of reality due the relative inexperience of human history determining its actions contextualized against the ranging scope of current experience, a present and past state melded with its exhibiting penalties and apathetic devotions not much further advanced in fathoming individualized distinction beyond rewarding humankind for its purported skilled victories over a planet and its common nature.

This event occurs in the present state of a reality, during an era of abundant data, science and claims on freedoms and awarenesses due the progressive evolution of humanity's unwitting accumulation of disproportionate latent knowledges it contagiously extracted as origin and erosion of its environment.

There should have been shamanic mystics, originators, leaders, sceptics and artists, unsolicited by the myriad of potential niche atmospheres they would have been unwittingly born into as the means to an end for rudely acceptable neurotypical ingenuities of imagination, beliefs of unkind insights, and plentiful self-appeasements.

Also, they should have been punished, segregated, shamed and medicated as discipline through the commands of a normalized mode of thinking, confining its undying depiction through the disassociated approaches and services executing an allistic-dominated human history with its slew of famous perpetrators.

These forceful old costumes of history persistently remain, directing human choices in the present state of the world, as diagnosed through the focusses of a moveable aspergic lens upon reality.

~~

Due to ineptitudes within the spectrum of knowledge instituted across unfamiliar generations of history, attitudes of the past cultivate an instinctive social dichotomy within those aspergic persons undiagnosed and misrepresented, existing in countless historical milieus, during recent and current times as an enigmatic, metamorphic wanderer and rebellious influencer upon budding embryonic symptoms within the spectrum of reality as it is associated with human social history, hardly counted among countless localized reoccurrences nudging its evolutionary attentions in jointly new and lost directions.

Unless a personality is fully consumed in repressive imitation and disguise accorded the stringent principles of social enactivism, an aspergic awareness observes the experiences and the makings of reality's symmetries as if mystical, or the convergent impression of beauty as if an observable ingredient of lighted, surfacing and nonphysical exhibitions emanating as the guarded modesty of nature; or the summation of aspergic identity enacted through the seeking and retention of lively patterned associations inclusive of nonphysical manifestations naturally cultivated from reality.

An aspergic individual does not naturally see peoples or nations, except as humanity and reality. The aspergic tendency is a willful attempt to find order in humanity's emotively complicated disorder, and the world's social and intellectual means as a frustrated, driving need for communal solutions beyond the indulgences of the ego-self as an individuality within highly populated groupings, rather than as an internalized illustration of unbiased empathy due the curtailment of aspergic identity as if desperate, rebellious avoidance is an only ready solution.

This attempt at escape is often redeemed as a losing surrender of one attached reality in favor of another attached reality reciprocally isolated in context whether in a rallying human arena or a secluded natural space. In either case, the sense of detachment is the same, in whichever experienced alternative of action is acted upon, so that any idea of escape entails nothing more excessive than a change in perceiving surroundings as an influence of direction and revolution of desires.

Nature is emotively releasing for its innovative sincerity upon aspergic susceptibilities, as if by identification mutually recognized in common, and as a separation given a human-instilled withdrawal from the past and future as relevance to an occurring present world. Nature is proof of truths not found or else lost within the human surreal, idealist spirituality, in favor of other purer symbols and actions rooted in embedded, private or esoteric beliefs and ravings.

It is difficult for a normal thinking mind to understand why an aspergic person would not want to adapt to the allistic-favored world and its many acceptable and contented benefits.

It is difficult for a normally emotive, bodily astute mind to fathom how an aspergic person should remain as unfitted for the world it seemingly rebuffs to the point of revolt across the spectrum of a lifetime, as an accurately fitting, chosen response while arrogantly rejecting the commoning, welcoming gesticulations of surreal opinions.

If everyone else generally behaves with solemn believability according to conformed ideals, then it can be confounding why an aspergic individual would not want to become closer to those communicative influences through acting like or preferably learning to appropriately imitate such a world it finds inherently difficult to appreciate, and a condition of personality repressible for reciprocal betterment to individual and the greater allistic majority.

As with evolution, the societal world desperately seeks better solutions to further its evolutions, with an equated range of deniability and comprehensions much as with species facing changing environments, whether composed of an original, bodily or mindfully surreal world.

The prism of aspergic beliefs views a world both real and surreal, riding the stormy waves between the two realms of manifested truths.

Aspergic sensitivities readily intuit the natural world with capacity for reaching far greater depth than the incongruity of a distracted humanity due to a likely proficiency to focus, to single out and associate, like predator to prey, momentary experiences of realness within surprising, unpredictable, surging instances of merging contexts, through the valuations of unmasked evidences and senses of reality found plainly hiding as rare but discoverable, lucky gifts.

~~

Over the range of a lifetime, an aspergic individual can consume inordinate amounts of energy stubbornly trying to rightfully prove oneself valid against a backdrop of self-doubting sureness instilled by an inversely composed world forced into unsolicited contention by the forces of universal evolution.

In a world ripe with fruitful revelations, the aspergic attention can come to limit what it reveals to the world due the recognition of risk at what cannot be sufficiently gauged by a disinterested, allistic-persuaded world, yet be completely haunted of a diverse empathy, more inclusive and less outwardly animated than other divergent, bodily endowed, intimidating personas found through the temptations of reality continuing the reoccurring compulsion of past generational abundances of successes through unconsented aggressions.

It is difficult to find true empathy in allistic-determined worldly actions and acceptability, no different than it can be exceedingly unimpressive when encountering the reactions of an aspergic mindset enabled with such pure sensitivities but instead outwardly imitating the surfaced surreality according to its enhanced powers of regulated culturing, thereby merely impersonating the rest of the world in its replication of allistic-determined compassions.

Such minds can be vulnerable to losing a contextual identity of private empathy due to disenchantment of the external, normalized reality, making it contend with the world as if burdened with seeking consent for such abstract, genetically-enhanced insensitivity rarely otherwise found to experience except through the motives of personal involvements mutely exposed to the enabling aftermaths of surreality in its countless past and current enactments, churning its justifications founded on an original ignorance, furthering its rallying opportunities for advantage.

The aspergic individual is compelled to explore the thresholds and boundaries of reality, to push outcomes, stirring up new descriptions in its pursuit of testing the murkiness of its environment for essential feedback.

The aspergic individual is given the choice to assume and be consumed by normalcy, or carefully embrace the non-normal sensitivities afforded by a separate way of thinking, feeling and sensing the world. There is recognition these differing sensitivities, same as with nonhuman species in its originally landscaped world, can share the manifold points of view as willful appreciation of the spectacle of varied awarenesses vital for an overwhelming, far-reaching success of global survival.

A diversity of experiences is essential to a relationship showing associations of patterned thinking gotten through a striven, emotively advanced learning requiring the detection, avoidance and corrections of individual errors as an accumulated, kept new attention to reality. Aspergians are forced to learn to tolerantly get along with regularized insights and tempered ideas as the methods of allistic-inspired survival, even if it only applies superficially and with applied caution as true inspiration from the quietude of an aspergic perspective.

Within these individuals, normalized and victimized by the inborn chance accident of an allistic-designed reality, the inner world can be an unaware conflict of differing perspectives, patterns of understanding and depth of associations versus what is normalized as *acceptance* in others when it comes to understanding justification for behaviors and the customary, worn methods of ready opinions of reality. It can become difficult to reconcile what is intuitively perceived distinctively within the natural world with the surreal edifice of humanity attempting to raise itself above it from its starting ill-informed, absent awareness founded on instinctive cognizance and a varied, spittled environment of pristine, contending symbolic aspirations provisioned for its newfound consciousness to become seeking and playful.

~~

Among individuals the differing awarenesses can blend and appear seamless when the influence of an external supplementary world allows a normalization of aspergic personalities to glow and freely, persuasively texture a reality.

Aspergic tendencies are one small aspect of the spectrum of personality, or the spectrum of reality's coalescing forces, or the spectrum of awarenesses among nonhuman species, and the measured spectrum of dominance within environments. Among all these coalescing spectrums of a world, the allistic interpretation is contended as physically and spiritually absolute, and as best fitted for challenging this willing, defenselessly consensual natural world, with its corresponding universal forces harmoniously scaled as equivalent to the energy of infinity versus a planetary speck of existence. This scale corresponds to the dense, speck-like stimulation of aspergic persuasions enacting change upon the loud momentum of an assaulted, allistic-concepted world-ordered history.

· The Spectrum of Personality

The spectrum of personality allows the accumulation of a range of permissible talents, skilled awarenesses, diverse acceptances, and intended beliefs. With aspergic tendencies pulsing within an individual's desire for better identity, a force must be exerted and accepted as received before it can be of meaning, thereby creating a response in return. In a way, social energy can only be spent if fittingly absorbed from outside beforehand. Initiatory action is limited as viable alternatives for aspergic individuals, reflecting best as a social success when balanced between identity and environment, usually occurring as localized comforts between intervals of discomforts with others less uniform in reciprocal responses – or essentially contrary or unempathetic personalities – and the coincidence of being occasionally, sedately removed from solitude through another person, people, nature or environment as a reprieve.

The allistic personalities include within its divorcement from natural reality a wide range of variables and potentials in its quest for successes, so long as a conscience is cleanly appeased through a provision of accountable networks of beliefs including the basest self-rightfulness. The question can arise whether this absence of variety qualifies as best fitness within a socially believing and acting species among many species sharing a closed environment atop a bubble of reality.

The aspergic individual can come to observe the motivated consequences of history as having created a self-fulfilling scenario, especially growing over recent millennia, into a reality where the allistic personality determines the future course for all of nature and humanity due to its prior predatory successes of physical feats of dominance, and its pleasingly rewarding detachment from integrity versus alternate, contrary originalities of an overabundant world ready to be willfully sown.

Individuals of many cultures will choose to forcibly adopt abrasive, dominating and narcissistic personalities, primal behaviorisms as believably acceptable, promoting the standardizing of these personalities far more prevalently damaging to the course of human history as determined, disintegrated motivations for enlightened attainment.

Aspergic persons can naturally question such motives within the world as readily unfitting, as demanding an unattainable forgiveness, but often seem to act alone in this quest for insight.

~~

Aspergic tendencies can arise within a small part of an advanced conscious species, and a small part of those learn to express and reflect it with any pronounced skill. The reason is genuinely a lack of environmental knowledge, opportunity, or interest, and the unnerving tendencies exuded by surrounding, excitable types of personalities, equally constrained by their own dilemma of mind, and often forceful in opposition to relinquishing an original, misconstrued ignorance of humanity as a fitting mystical origin.

For innumerable generations, aspergic tendencies walked unnoticed, unrecognized, given to a normalized, allistic deniability in recognition of difference among regulated traits of personalities. Humanity didn't have much interest in personalities except as forceful appeasement to an associated reflection of iconic status within its natural milieu; and as fodder for new arising personalities to reassume. Accordingly, the characteristics of advantage in these tendencies have been accepted and integrated according to the urgency of its qualifications within goading allistic aspirations, predetermined tolerances permittable to allistic successes, thereby revealing many genuine impulses of allistic self-bias in its wake.

In this context, aspergic tendencies show resistance as an interpretation challenging to the true idealized beliefs of reality contained within the believable imaginings of its species. Without a sense of overwhelming justness, the aspergic identity has difficulty pursuing the mainstream as an ideal representation of the world, instead of as a mired world counter-resisted in agreement.

~~

Like many conditions of personality, the aspergic individual must learn and practice facing a given reality without private segregation, as loss of experiences against other differing groups or conditions of personality. This is a reciprocal gain since the allistic mindset must learn to cope with differing interpreted sensitivities of reality other than its unchecked original pride. Otherwise, there is mutual inexperience especially during younger ages leading to the same repeating behaviors in adulthood without reciprocal gain in understanding other than through conflicted resistance due an equalized mistrust.

Aspergians and other minority personas throughout history will have contributed to the benefit of the allistic world's dominant stance. Though difficult to quantify the contribution, the absence of these scattered insights, ingenuities, alternative patterns of perceptual talents should have limiting and impressive consequences on the shape of the current state of such ready-made world, perhaps to its unwitting culpability as contributor to an unbound allistic reality unconstrained by genetic integrity.

A growing awareness of aspergic realization expressed through its tendencies creates a moral dilemma concerning the difficulty with passing on genes. Observing a plainly viewable world of surrounding experiences and the consequences to personal identities and social dynamics in the trivial details holding its totality, it can seem unconscionable to further a genetic journey. It becomes difficult to ascertain which is a worse world for an offspring, allistic or aspergic in context, and whether the aspergic individual can decide or make such a punishing choice for a future offspring to have to imprison within such an illusory, hardened reality.

Aspergic persons look for truths, the right and wrong of an event or situation such as humanity on a planet, its implications, impressions and deniability, not wanting to act on falseness or pretense as a contributor to furthering an existing misdirection.

For reasons of identity and the integrity of having to difficultly live with oneself and one's consequences with heightened recall and conscience, as the workings of an inner self-making, aspergic persons cannot as easily become corrupted in status or personality. In this way, they can be inspiring for their impressive persona of an exaggerated kind of normality, though this exaggeration only exists due the contrasting unseen exaggerations of normalcy due the allistic identities.

Perspectives of the aspergic experience as an aspect of human history apply to all contrary perspectives of feelings and beliefs among humans and nonhumans diluted in relevance against the dominance of a rallying allistic viewpoint.

There are certain to be varying marks and stimuluses throughout history of such aspergic tendencies; defined as a condition, such a thing would not just abruptly stop or occur in a species with such an absorbing capacity of imitating personality traits coaxingly enhanced by the persuasions of environments.

~~

Allistic identities can be limited in focused attentions, intentions and skills the same as aspergic minds and bodies tend towards multiple interests of useful skills and practiced levels of skills depending on the motivations enabling a repeating willingness of pursuit. It is the hunt or success of the seeking which is limiting due to success being externally conceived more as a failure compared to an overcompensated expansion of allistic attentions as priority. This can create an underachieving individual as a means of fitting in or dumbing down as a relationship with the world it needs for sustenance the same as any allistic-tempered person.

~~

At any point in the history of advancing an informed cognizance founded on empirical understandings of minds and emotional responses to complexities of being, with individual responses to a reality's replies to its societal stages of understandings and coinciding misunderstandings with each new stage of betterment, not just of the abstract obscurity of self in the face of an agonizing awareness of existence and the frustrated limits of grasping this seemingly unfathomable hiddenness, it can be seemingly normal to avoid this vastness in favor of a subdued or extravagantly misled, self-imaged personality.

Through the sluggish evolution of history's understanding of knowledge, these resentful conflicts have been absorbed by a storied humanity and nonhumanity, multiply exposed to a hard reality for such minds to fully grasp and accept, yet to intuit with high awareness something lost or never found due to an off-centered loss of imagination.

Normalcy in this World

The natural world promotes diversity among species within environments and among individuals within species. This variation allows limited behavioral freedoms through a genetic exhibition within reality promoting subtle differences according to physical capabilities and local variations of environment. As a consciousness grows within a species as a deterrent for better survival, there are extended residual emergences from these communicative idiosyncrasies: as a consciousness begins not to shape niches but construct them as a diversity of appearance, taking on in struggle and resistance the entropic reality it initiates its new surreality upon as a backdrop of symbol, memory, convenience of use, and the underwhelming condition of its resistance to overwhelming will and force.

The natural world, it is learned through adaptation, can be readily outwitted by a properly evolved bodily shape with a coinciding clever, predicting mind. Within an unconscionable species with the conscious will and bodily capability to shape reality to its bidding, nature is vulnerable. This inscrutable will exists within a bubble of disorganized and incomplete ideas without much overall aptitude for understanding future outcomes as a forceful, mainstream independence of hungered obesity as its surviving ambitious desire for overindulgences.

To observe the real and surreal worlds in contrast and with contesting juxtaposition, a world where true integrities are disregarded in favor of opinioned views of reality, where differing perspectives are irrelevantly treated and acted upon through a resentful commonness of individual personalities untrained for the natural world of existence to foster higher measures of command and confidence standing before successful innovated, celestial landscapes, as witness to the natured personas of an open-minded universe segregated as a species from favoring a practical mindfulness empty of true mystical, coincidental and natural connotations.

Normal is not erasing the present from the future as experience. It is not omitting this experience from unnamed others, from oncoming generations. It is not removing the temptations for awe from the world. It is not the end of the believable within the imagination of humanity as a spiritual and physical wholeness in isolation, rather than the opportunity at diverse enlightenment it ceaselessly afforded overlooking.

2.   Stratagem Disguised as Rule and Experience

Gameplaying can be interpreted as an unsurprising, forceful, and fluidly surfacing obligation within the world's evolutionary shifts among diverse species of predation and competitors for niche solutions. To successfully advance in the contest of evolution, it was budding, promising and selected as a vital, inviting emergence of the fine-tuned and exhaustive improvement of regulated traits as a bourgeoning, identifying validity among the ever-growing expanse of species on a planet.

The designs, parameters and rules of the game are afforded by the forces of the universe previously established before the convergence of life emerged as a new force from a precedingly strewn beginning: from a backdrop of unobserved, energized reality into which life could symmetrically attach and appear with the unavoidable, inexperienced, unrelenting compulsion to play along as an only means of achieving fulfillment of survival's continued betterment, its enhancing focus of attentions and the surfacing of latent talents pronounced through skilled shapes and bodily persistence as a scheme of niche fitness.

To not play along is to not learn, to not extend the unique collections of sensory readiness, predictability and the willing adaption necessitated to successfully evolve; or else to be consumed and replenished by new as yet unrealized challengers eager for a chance at entering the immense contest of players competing for niche allotments. These victories bestow the rewards of new successful abilities within a contending species ripe for further play with the confidence of a defined subjugator of personal niche space and as a continued occurrence as a winning player within the scenarios of the game's future.

Through a clever approach to this natural and lethal drama, tallness and prominent physical composition do not obligate victory over more diminutive species and the amassed ranges of strategic potentials contained within its reality unburdened by immensity and shaped by differently perceptive, intended commands of forces.

The exploration of niches is perceived through the outcomes of successful maneuvers organized through established, practiced behaviors and confined genetic routines, the competition of winning evidence against other local and non-local species, organisms and communally created environments playing the same game of survival based on the universal forces they each share as mutual context and gameboard for discovery and invention of stratagem.

The playing fields transformed into distinctive landscapes through predatory movements and attainment of ever newer multidimensional solutions from an originally insensitive environment to one teeming with insights and cognizant endeavors of improvement, continually striving towards ever-greater victories of success and new subsequent awarenesses for this deliberately acting world of malleable traits, designs and the surfacing of winning behaviors achieved from an originating manipulation of felt unseen forces acted upon to reshape the prior embryonic backdrops.

As an outcome of the playing environments developed through its feats of triumph, gameplaying follows an advancing scale of manipulation, ploy and primary consequences as far back as the level of cells as descriptive resources of confined ingenuity. It is conceivable to be applied to the level of particle, wave, force and field as a pondering evolution into a workable universe capable of substantiality and inclusive of primal environments skilled at prospecting life through the force of gelling evolutionary transformation.

~~

The veracity of winning in the game becomes what can be realized and gotten away with by whatever reachable innovations, resources and dimensions afforded as guided paths towards embedded evolutionary transformations; and the acclaimed feat of entering the game as a player by becoming a distinctly competent species within a niche.

The cleverness of skills, the substance and reflection of overawing, antagonistic intentions, verbosity, posturing and disinterest unavoidably become growingly rewarded victories within the surreal world of humanity where it found such benign attainments useful within the originating world of nature accorded to the simple originalities and native restrictions of reality's subversive contests for niche dominance.

Reciprocally, the unconscious traits of a prior landscape of reality released through the human conscious interpretation during a progressively innovative future state, such as occurred over the preceding few millennia, can become perverted by greed of rewards, replicating natural successes with dexterous fingers and adventurous imaginings seeking a vindication not otherwise found within nature as an overshadowing, separate, dominating intention: as reachable self-evidence against the validity of all other niche-empowered environments of a planet as a dramatic exhibition of true, conflicting solidarity in consummated, coordinated stratagem.

Higher potentials within subsequent complexities of cognizant awarenesses and contradictory patterns of reality do confront genuine, realizable and emotive loss as a subsequent defiance against this newfound, unconscionable and evolving willpower to furthering human discipline as a shadowed belief within reality, with each species either opposed or obliging to new symbiotic environments attuned through the sensitivities and willpowers of all species as a competing conjunction, endlessly chasing the transformations of nature's environments alongside the surrendering of old and attaining of new niche markers.

A widely affectionate contempt of nature is thought to be redeemed through the advent of humanity and the furthering of its success as a superior, all-encompassed last solution to a deep, fine and infinitely detailed universe.

Humanity, as a last solution, perceives of itself victory over a planet, over evolution, above reason and cause, and in full, proud belief of its placed, allotted role as the obvious end-victor and best answer for the sake of the observable universe.

~~

Within the arena of nature, as a restraining rule of the game, success is not all-consuming and permitted a confinement to one niche fulfillment as a dominant, ruling solution for all if victory is to be lasting and not otherwise absent as a force within a welcoming environmental cohesiveness.

The environment must succeed alongside the victors, whether a singularity or multiplicity of continuing attainment. No one species in a natural world dominates in its relationship with all other essential organic niches through unification into one all-consuming niche.

Due the certain silence of a spiritual awarenesses composed of unique sensitivities of reality, this world cannot exist within the scope of a singular collective awareness doomed by isolation without a proper measure of environmental sustenance and its invigorating diversity of associations. One species concocting upon nature a persevering martyrdom and omission in deliberation, or the heedful quest and sought promise of a future model for the perfected, succeeded regulation of nature by its defter hands as an endgame, is a doable solution for a potential species as a short-lived, unsighted triumph utilizing the surfacing power of pride instilled by its original, lasting inexperience.

Humanity assumes a bullying attitude towards an objectified, mocked nature as an amusing, soulless thing beneath a soulful, spirited, meaningful humanity. Humanity assumes the supremacy of its meaning above all others for the sake of its willing reasonableness to make it an obvious truth in a world where previously truth had never been a factor other than change and consequence due evolutionary victors and losers.

The invention of truth within the universe is for playful endeavors with far-reaching tendrils opportune for stratagem, made for clever minds unencumbered by integrity and the processes embedded in environments through expanding conformations of manifold justness, as awakened beliefs beyond mere truth as a usefulness.

Humanity assumes its truth and its meaning as a symbolized restructuring of nature fit for its use of belief, as the discovering conqueror of truth above all other quieter interpretations of the universe ranging the world in multitudes of variety plentifully everywhere it looked and ventured to walk since its original, proud gamble out of the trees, unwittingly ready to undo an unsuspecting and strangely whispering reality.

As with multitudes of peoples under clever and hard-fought capitulation, nature quietly must adhere and defer to the idea of the perfect fusion of mind and body as fitting the successes of humanity accidentally shaped as the dualistic and sensitive personification of celestial, god-imaged spirituality within the universe.

Human spirituality, its enlightenment, its solemn arrival as the last solution in full, proud belief of itself: humanity has shaped the universe in its image with the self-assured certitude of an approaching game-winning victory.

Nature does not otherwise assume an isolated entity of dominant manifestation within the universe, or at least within an isolated, local solar system remote from further environmental sustenance for its evolutionary branches to reach into the patterned light of the universe.

If there were earlier, primal attempts at overwhelming success at the expense of all other species atop a planet, its long-serving absence of occurrence during any current epoch of its future such as the present *now* of this world should admit its failure to achieve any ambitions of whole, fulfilling dominance against the ambitions of wide-ranging, shared diversity as a better overwhelming solution.

~~

Before the arrival of the human species as a surfacing product of nature, wanton greed of removing deviating gameplaying solutions was skillfully contained by nature over eons of predatory millennia by systems unifying the equilibrium of bodily energy and consumption essentials to peaks of coexisting symmetry. These experiences were aligned with the familiarity inspired within regulated genetic memories of the solutions through traits to environmental provocations. These solutions produced the constrictions of behaviors and shapes of countless species through the later and merciless games being locally played atop a planet for countless generations of predatory change and its innovating improvements into flourishment.

Inevitably, success breeds higher realizations, solutions and truths of reality which must be risked through the chance improvement of a conscious cooperative of awarenesses. This is a hefty risk for nature to assume for the reason of the probable loss of boundary, control and the promise of an overwhelming thrill of dominance occurring as a confused, willful choice within a newly rationalizing species.

This attentive species, a product of the interconnecting experiences of all prior life, inclusive of the countless species submerged within the planet's encrusted deposits of mistaken or misleading, unsuccessful or merely progressively strategic pathways of contribution to furthering evolution's gameness and length of field upon which to play.

The innovations of this otherwise illusive species until the point of its upright appearance walking from the waters, mountains and trees, its enthusiasms for improvement through its exhibited, ruthless gameplay of hereditary survival, were ruled by the forces of reality procuring a diversely immersive landscape for it to cling to like a branch holding its finding awareness aloft above an otherwise endless, utter unawareness, and the game is lost. An unawareness like the effect on this planet and solar system if the universe were to suddenly become unappealing to gravity. The instant contraction of gravity's absence would instantly spiritually absolve all physicality of its material suffering into an empty, merely imaginable poof of dust opening into an empty, deprived hollowness.

Without these prior forces, there would be no choice of dominance among species, no extinction or rediscovery of species, no conception of a potential nonexistence, and no ideas of surrender and transgressive acceptance of a hungered spirituality in need of sating beliefs. Among individuals of a sentient species, there can be proffered the option of self-exploitation, of perpetrating a con against an unwitting worldly awareness procured through naïve eternities of striving towards better prediction of solutions accorded the rules and scheming play of nature's inspiring, well-rewarded, predatory games.

For this new species, these predictable repercussions spread into all undulations of truths plucked from reality's moveable texture, so that the verity contained within solutions of nature became disguised as motivating powers, as an exalted, inheritably unachievable greatness idolized as beginning, as meaning and persistence, as intention and willful pride of action, and as a playing field ripely fit for diverse conflict.

The inevitable arrival of these historical compromises with reality emanates from the simple successes of traits for betterment and survival among assorted species of life struggling to organize niche conceptions of mind, body and environment into well-adjusted stratagems. Inevitably, with helpful conditions and an innovative evolutionary energy, there ascends the appearance of a functioning planet teeming with life-filled victory and success of solutions among an incredible range of deeply textured environmental realities.

Fitness is not monopolized by any one or few species, but as accumulations of shared attributes and the occurring manifestations of these many accumulations alongside the resultant predatory niche developments shaping the reality shared and composed through incalculable divergent comprehensions. Each identity of species is a distinctive property and exhibition of a realized, successful universe behaving as a stable, current summation of solutions on demonstration for all life to find in proper awe-like obligation of benefit.

~~

The contributions of traits extracted as mechanisms of gameplay within the natural world become regressed and debauched methods of amusement and self-confirmation within the new surreal world of humanity constructed in its stead. Its growing complexity procures new, differing material tenacities for sensitive bodies, aware minds and the cultured responses produced through believable behaviorisms enhanced by conforming scale and escalating values of attention and deniability beyond the range of a surreal environment's coaxing surrender to further explanation. Its ghostly coexistence is like an endgame won and consigned to persist as a sole residual system to efficiently aid further a sole species bent upon excelling the savoring blisses of its hereditary rush.

Deniability is helped by the loss of attraction to reality, of obscured, unfocussed minds acting in conjunction within a limiting, restraining niche environment promoting such values as promising and worthy of attachment for successes otherwise believed absent as survivability.

Localized environments limit and enhance the advance of gameplay solutions due to an incomplete scope of understanding the universe among the many singular and conjoined niche comprehensions of its species in relationship with all others, while the many localized environments inevitably, broadly overlap as newer solutions are continually sought and imaginatively sown.

Deniability is a quality of the natural world usurped and evolved by the new surreal world. Species cannot act on every occurrence occupying their perceptions as if reality were a feast of preoccupation rather than a game towards utter dominance as a succeeding species among many species, achieved through niche selection including focus, attention and confidence in skills.

Species become contained within the realm of comprehended niches allowing the survival of generations worth of hoarded enlightenments. This previsioning permits better access to survival as the current representation of a gathered history imprinted within each cell of each member's body and mind convincing it to act appropriately unless otherwise stressed or forced into new areas of betterment or skill in its gameplay tactics.

~~

Inevitably, the natural world becomes so distinguished with gameplaying solutions it ceases to be much of a game as niche fulfillment of winning players become unwittingly, mutually entrenched within uncountable thickly layered environments. A tolerance of other combining successes prevails within an equalizing peripheral world allotted the eons to advance its gameplaying skills as a coinciding, sacrificial force for betterment. The world becomes a blend of conquerors segregated as species each acting and behaving in confident mutuality through niche communities within many localized milieus. This concurring feat of abundant temporal experience coats a planet in the comfort of a bright, energized and wide-arching triumph.

An eventual, overwhelming victory lasts until a consciously unified, willful awareness, generated as a newfound sequence of solutions surfacing from the world of solutions and the promise of immediate and lasting benefit, appears as a better choice of fitness, as a regulator of more hits and wily, unabashed swelling battles of wills against a world of nature brimming and enclosing a planet fully with a vastness of wrought and contented fitness in overabundant sureness.

A world of communal mindfulness generously endowed to the new salivating awareness within humanity assumes limited to no residual relationship with its underlying natural world except as camouflage, and the ingenuity or encouragement of appropriately satisfying, projected human spiritual alertness.

As the victor claiming the right of exclusive spiritual actuality upon the world, humanity gained multilayered access to the afterworld of its conception duly fitted for the human soul. For the first instance within a vast universe, a meaning had been uttered through human spiritual recognition as seen and found according to the evolving awareness bestowed by consciousness and its unquestionably entangled hunger for self-advantaging beliefs.

This shift in sensitivity made of the dispirited old world an observable wonder and mystical inspiration for the betterment of human physicality and chronicled, documented spirituality in the new world.

A conscious species might assume the bewilderment of deniability, easily afforded by the seeming voiceless rapport of reality and the natural world as a selected affinity, for better survival avoiding bodily and mindful dysfunction as species can succumb to as a lost or vacated niche formally comprehended and fitted is lost. Instead, as a surviving species to live, celebrate and idolize deniability to overabundance as a claimed right with the attention of self-wonder before a common world.

In nature, deniability is niche acceptance and its motivating invigoration on normalizing behaviors; in the surreal world, deniability is the regression of instinctive values and the discarding with natural basis as a factor in favor of idled, usurped remedies to an unprovable meaning of existence. It is the condoning of this lack of meaning as the foundation for transgressions against an inurned opinion of exempted spirituality in nature, and the phantasm of substituted, prismatic beliefs in its newfound intention for one exclusive, mystically imaginative species.

This deniability can be tempered on a scale which is unflinching in its restful integrity as fisted solution. Being completely, naturally obtainable, contrived and malleable, it is a perfected tool with abiding uses. History proves the corruptibility of humanity, that it is not to be fully trusted, especially within the limited confines of any single human being and what might be expected of such a corrupted byproduct within the overarching design of reality and the encouraging power it might impose upon masses of individuals. The species could not fast from this unrelenting temptation for rule as a bending source of abundance, so it should not be generally expected from individuals as the originators, culprits and victims of jointly satisfying stratagems freshly reoccurring over a mainstream of historical perspectives.

Coincidentally, the makeup of reality does allow this potential fasting of abusive sensitivities in a shortage of rebellious individuals as a focused experience of identity in behaviors and actions against a crushing juxtaposed world of conformism. These fewer, balanced individuals would be motivated to further or better the future world as lifelong, unannounced self-request. Without the impervious conformity of multitudes, rebellious spirits would find no fit environment or cause to surface as force other than as a merely latent stimulus upon the world of improvement.

Generally, the return to nature or nativity as a new wellspring of spirituality and guidance, as a protector of a different justness, as a selfless choice for greater betterment, becomes a strangely aggressive, disobedient pursuit against the healthier interests of a wider humanity and its unquestioning historical contexts of favored beliefs.

~~

In the past and current worlds, to learn to participate without the practice of gameplay, without understanding its spirited strategies, urging potentials and intended abject solutions, without learning to skillfully create and find foreseeable innovation ready to utilize as necessitated by the moment, is to be put to disadvantage as a developing inhabitant of humanity or a retreating nonhuman entity or species.

Once, this gameplay only applied in its relationship with the natural world's localized, familiar and inherited environments, but through the socially complexing perspectives of fierce histories and subsequent raised resentments, with technological benefit overtaking the solutions once prescribed to bodily traits, it has become an essential component to survival in the human-made surreal world without having to surrender to nature as an inflexible niche allotment alongside others in unified multiplicity.

Multiplicity within nature as a grander solution is conceived as a novice, primordially youthful game traversing the world of survival without much accumulation of personal experience or skills beyond the endowment from inheritances as a confined genetic starting point. The assumption of nature's unawareness and indifference to its fate is ironically undoubted. The niche realizations and conscious solutions substituting traits, rallying new behaviors and aware thinking for humanity inevitably to become all-consuming and wide-ranging in benefitting solutions, absent much further innovative integrity of spirit.

~~

In gameplaying situations, the loss of advantage or consistency coming from being unpracticed can be itself a ploy by another for its self-advantage and winning strategy, especially as a handed remnant of the past's convergent power solutions for localities and populations.

In cases of birthright, the disadvantage of this inhibiting style of environmental allowance upon individuals and peoples within an evolving, dynamic, and past-bound reality can leave most at the drawback of starting the game as the victim of inherited strategies poorly devised; or a lack of success merely through historical capitulation to dominant-hungered strategies within the local environment it coincidentally was born into as a new reality tangled and bound to all the old ones as determined.

These environments are equipped and the weakened burdened by the designs of the gameplaying world to previously inspire it, without much chance to overcome the conditions of inherited, perpetrated tactics and its accepted adoptions as chronicled rules and demands; embedded within these same inherited localized worlds of whispered meanings, scaled to the life-imposed values of a new environmental framework, advanced through the relic solutions of contested, historized decisions prevalent in the present world as the spiteful, mocking haunt of a willful force exuded and sustained as an impressively preserved ritual and ceremony within the conditions of abject acceptability.

~~

The necessitating nature of knowledge and consciousness is the *idea* of the world versus its *reality*, or the disinformation which naturally occurs from information, of its command and circulation among multitudes of highly susceptible individuals enthusiastic for ready and affordable strategies of new self-appeasement.

The games are perpetuating, with each new generation of individuals needing to rediscover the experiences for themselves anew however many times the similar practice has been had and repeated by countless others in the past in differing contexts and contrasts of exhibition, so that the textures and subtle nuances of fine-tuned reexperience is exhaustingly explored for higher solution and benefit.

Many of these reexperiences are dire in intention creating resentful human and nonhuman victims of human deniability as a newly surfaced awareness of the true bounds of contorted consciousness is countlessly explored for advantage, and the calculated thresholds of willfulness to assume contagious beliefs are uncovered and favorably associated within the networks of human reality.

~~

Occurring throughout much of civilized history, this approach to reality becomes a singular attribute of humanity or a convergent yearning of human consciousness in many environments of the same world, as a likely sculpting of the melded forces acting upon it, permissible through a cognizant aptitude of mutually competing survival as risks, rewards and detriments constrained by the boundaries of scarcely conceived, imposed universal dynamisms.

There exists the marked predatory maneuver of playfully regulating the occurrences of resolve upon earlier and later unfounded beliefs and feelings within collaborators. This playful scenario occurs as a direct intention against a marked vulnerability in spiritual confusion and valued satiety of alleged soul once sufficiently belief-enthused within enough historized participants. In this scenario, belief is not found but given as a provision and commodity, and the idea of its necessity for genuine sustenance and unassailing devotion ripe within the physical world of a surreal-minded humanity.

This devotion to spiritual satiety often leads to the instilled habit of comforted sameness with fellow partakers, while accepting the confounding sense that delinquency of conduct and endgame strategies are tolerable if it helps the self's group as a primary fitting success.

This duplicitous thinking is not moral thinking since any natural conception of morality is shaped by the expected multiplicity captured within a species exacerbated by a seemingly advancing knowledge of conscious responsiveness and enhancing focus, with its processes of emotively thoughtful responses mimicking the preconceived methods of solution reflected in evolution as diversity and the niche innovations within manifold natures of concentrated awarenesses.

~~

As a species, humankind has learned, as a means of better solutions, to disguise itself from nature, stepping out of its skin with an intent on shedding evolution from its future as a further, peaking realization. A species of individuals are mutually disguised in the full spectrum of observation before nature and its celestial eternity, unafraid of admitting what cannot be recognized, unafraid of its limitless inexperience, and its hollow enlightenment for the horror of spiritual interpretation within a freshly correlating mind; instead, finding it as a confidence beneath the disguise, deriding the natural world and the cosmos for its nakedness.

These disguises of character create a surreal world living atop the old real world of nature and existence as a discordance and convenient, communal denial.

The disguises are costumes of mind and behaviorisms of personalities in a firmly established environment. They are the mimicking of fitness for the mind to endure its new world no different than the disguises of mind, skins, furs, clothes, shells and manipulated light found in nature permitting the continued surviving longevity of its untiring inundation of overflowing species for so long.

~~

Throughout human history, there is the progressive beautification of self, the virtue of self, the power and will of an identifying personality mutually among the array of other seekers of the same identification. It is naturally peculiar to assume such will and design upon and for no grander motive than oneself among multitudes of others doing the same as an endgame of the universe.

This can be attributed to a natural lacking within reality, its absence of certitude in direction or practical guidance otherwise without adhering the interpretations of an intuitively silent nature and cosmos observably hollow of any other plain answer or unifying meaning, contrasted to the plentiful answerabilities of surreality. This occurs among a backdrop in which many inevitably no longer look to nature or the sky as finding source of promotional awareness.

Humanity, from an origin, is haunted by allegations of spirituality and the descriptions of chronological events within a world devalued by the unceasing surfacing of personalizing identity in a vaguely correlated reality, as humanity attempted the long process of overlooking and forgiving the natural world its usual disobediences.

The world of knowledge being equal to the world of spirit in value and urgency, it began from a foundation of unawareness, forcing the obligation of initial and compounding predictions, associations, symbols, and meanings discoverable as usable solutions for the manifestation of humanity's new ideas of the world. This fresh world originates as an inexperienced, absent spirit of the natural world attempting to survive the new associations of mind and body compelling it, much like cells regulating and producing proteins for active improvements, to find and construct better, materially substantive solutions.

Individuals prove the drive of individuality among a horde of other similar accumulations of intentions and survivals, concepts and beliefs about identity of actions through the echoing patterns of generational reality.

Life becomes for humankind a stratagem for the establishment of sequential rules and visions dictating the arguments for new streamlined experiences ready for concentrations of localized offspring to aspire or despair. Alleged redeemed solutions as something snatched from reality, as conscious workable disclosure from past inexperience, the transformation of nature and its impressions ensues through wills ravaged by the many processes meant to contain disinformation by fostering and recording it as ownership, as the striven measures for the supervision of spiritual beliefs about individuality and otherworldly losses and rewards as the means to further intimidating success in this world: as an old persuasive force or stratagem successfully lingering within the world of human stipulation, as a meaningfully projected determination and the regulating measures of synchronized guidance as benefit.

~~

As a facet of humankind's overexerted advancement as a willpower and individuality upon the world, acute individuals will come to perceive not only the present but the future as an intention, tendency and coincidence, finding it to be of greater importance than the urges of a faithless, unreliable present state.

Through force of subjugation in advancing absolute knowledge and spiritual values, individuals will leave personalized indications, ideas, contrary perceptive tendencies and conceptions of instruction or validation for the future to preferably grasp what a wavering present state of humankind as a historical era could not except within the imaginings of exclusive minds differently cognizant enough to predict and attempt to control it. These wills admit the futility of any lasting revolutionary conversion during the presented world of visibly unified inexperience claimed as a determined, unceasing present-day reality.

Within this scope of human descendancy of spiritual and contextual inheritance, there are acts of great purity and insight, and acts of great spite and retribution to be handed to recurring generations.

The future should come to inevitably, passionately sympathize with confident individuals of the past with admiration and recognition at how they at least attempted to benefit the future through envisioned communication, risky actions and zealous illustrations; and the many with alternate sensitivities who had to endure the worst atrocities of the continuous present state often dominated by a forceful will to punishment against the natural world of nature and clear-sighted attunement with the advantaged partiality of humanity.

Instead, humankind's clearly spiritual nature is arisen in the situation of its gleaning image as iconic motivation furthering the steadfast paths of intimidation and verdict found inherently embedded inside the making of current human and nonhuman reality.

~~

A species can unwittingly set itself along a path of eventual defeat by nature and its methods of longsuffering regrowth. Through attempts to banish empathy and inspiration with directed focus on an obscure mainstream end by whatever means, forced to admit to submission to the evidences of abstract leadership as the redeeming talents of personality, given a choice of unrealistic options, people will usually find the one which helplessly validates them utmost in the moment. Justification of immoral behaviors begins within the nature of personality and spreads through the reflections perceived by others as commonness.

To survey and study human history is to also realize the future's past potentially in the current world with an improved, unbiased predictability and a fresh dissociating sense of loyalty to that history. Understanding in others the ploy of manipulation, that to pity misfortune in another will shape and assume that pity within them as an identity of subjugation or revolt. It is the same with all else shaped from the peripheral force of experiences. As it occurs in nature with evolution, it can be mimicked to enhanced extent in humans beyond the origin of fitting intentions and rigorous solutions.

It could be argued that morality has its place within laws of nature, or epics of time, through its manifold descriptions of brutality, but nature and epics of time evolve the same as all else.

The castigating of a puritanical worldly acceptability in the mystical phantasms of true belief should inevitably be achieved through relative safety of societal ease, through the growths of understanding of its validity and misuses, through communal and individual self-passions and an unbending acceptance of mutuality within a discreet universe of human and nonhuman awarenesses.

~~

There is a discovered conception of spiritual meaning fitted to human consciousness from the natural world, an emergence of universal meaning endowed within the personas of humanity's participants.

Humankind exists as sole ownership and in assertive belief of its entitlement of spirituality, of soul, of awareness and passion, of emotive thought, raised at the expense of the reigning balance of a natural world, a natural universe, of limitless species established as a prior icon intended to be swiftly uprooted with elevating victory to humankind as a pride, to rid and adulterate its hard-fought and raging attainment in poised competition, just and worthy of expelling such dissenting spirit into submission and the oblivion of unawareness with an ease not applicable to integrity.

Humankind can exist to take on reality in all its facets as the wellspring of otherworldly trial, as the redeeming, arriving life-force and proper endowment for the future as the fulfilled, instinctive realization of a successful endgame strategy, a believable triumph over the physical and the spiritual worlds of reality prescribed, for lack of better alternative, through the interpreted representations of the natural world it reciprocally demeans as unintendedly antiquated, unfitting and randomly accidental in its tactical, strategic solutions, communications, emotive awarenesses, and spiritual values, as pawn atop the lush landscape of ranging mountains, forests and waters making up the vast closed fringes of its gameplaying fields.

3. Consequentially Derived Choices

In a world premeditated by past choices, there are dynamic aftermaths to individuals and the human species generationally acting, fittingly behaving, and scarcely knowing the reality they are made to be part of. Without much detection, the world of humankind repeatedly loiters while furthering its own predictions, without imaginative seekers of finer, better truths resting blatantly dormant, and its many participants stop admitting the underlying natural world as magnitude in its connotations as a living, breathing, responsive awareness. This undervalue in substantiality mostly occurs in favor of simply accepting the nearest local facsimile of iconic belief according to a benign allotment by birth.

This agreement occurs coincidentally or convergently among a diverse range of the human species with intended members grouped by historically distanced localities of both time and space. These originating distances limited devastations potentially and likely to be caused by minimalizing contacts with outside and competing human species, permitting familiarity to appease the shyness of members as settled recompense through its fitful mollification of populations of undeterred spirits living as the coordinated and genius wonderment of nature's exhibitionism.

With humanity's believable ideas of the world, this randomness, chance allotment, lottery or straw picking of spiritual and moral value worthy of honored actions appears lacking as a reliable target. It is worthy more as a mutual, common value marked by possessiveness and self-justification for the sake of locality and its deep-rooted, culturally social interpretations. It exists in awe of an otherwise absent or unpresentable unifying answer.

In these cases, coming from the same world and limited environment of the universe, these differences and resulting conflicts of distrust are symbolic in nature and through genetic grounding cultured accorded to prior achievements and pragmatic conceptions of local successes; not as an only path or means to success, but the one previously selected and retained due the conditions and events of the surrounding, mysteriously living and nonliving reality it evolved alongside.

These systems of beliefs inevitably become potential struggles of conciliation as the old means of holding value in spiritual management is overwhelmed and reinvented by the natural improvement of an evolving unification of multifaceted beliefs, the ensuing insights into the past which become revealed through higher understandings, and the reduction of the human fear of others accorded the inherent risks of trying to survive a stacked reality manifested as a natural world veiling another, inner, reclusive world of bestowing attention.

Sufficiently advanced, the human-tended world begins to be overcome by the sharing of spiritual and physical traits, with beliefs stored as psychological solutions through generations of choice-fueled moments during any present state of the evolved past and repeated until the present state of a perplexed world.

The amassing and detailing of chosen belief solutions among groups can be found to be similar if not chronologically coordinated through coinciding isolations and contacts of many localities of history in varied stages of conscious willingness and acceptances of reality. Sharing the same universe, world and environment of niche-constructed life, the similarities of structured beliefs will be culturally and artistically dissimilar, though the roots are constrained by the same urges of the same universal forces and spectacle of prismatic reality.

Humankind were presented, during any past moments and whatever the eventual outcomes to the present world, with the same or closely consistent environments of life, with the ingredients and materials to reshape into the implements from which to create, identify, decide and grow as a unified version of evolutionary culmination identical in valid attainment and indebtment to the natural world and the unified mutuality of nonhuman species acting in coincidence for so long adjacently together.

~~

This possessiveness given to beliefs and the restrictions of choices derived from prior chronological punishments is a lingering remnant of a closed, isolated world preserving its boundaries of assorted claimed ownerships. As these boundaries of distance temporally dissolve, they become defensively reinforced through overlapping contacts into what is finally disclosed as a vast allotment of localized, environmentally and historically founded belief systems and humankind's reclusive, entitled revelation of an enduring spectrum of multifaceted mysticism, placing itself as a celestial epitome or center presiding in a present state of the world in every occurrence and all experiences as a gifted rapport. The notion of humanity spotted as a center of a universe is not far removed from antiquity within a current present reality due to its soothing successes upon the human awareness for its soulfulness as a descriptive and flattering mirrored self-image.

This unification could be an act of pride, gift and vision, or one of retreat in defense against an unavoidably approaching, closing future.

Given the undeniable choice in most cases of inevitable amalgamation, mystical isolationism and minority entitlement within clans and populations reaches a peak of success as a better solution. As with evolution, a change in trait or skill is never immediate within a species but takes many generations to become situated as a new surfacing property of its proceeding social reality.

A rational species, with a true measure of rationality, would view this inevitability as a natural movement; instead, humanity mainly perseveres by safeguarding outdated systems of beliefs as if a survivability depended upon it — which it often has as mutual self-fulfillment — but in actuality it is the current habitual labyrinth of past choices of survival as a best and only solution not to be reneged. The distrusting, unknowing risk of choice and the permanence of choices within other individuals and groups demanded enthusiasm for the past as the unswerving answer to the present.

Conformity to belief in the new evolution of ideas becomes resistance to the future for the betterment of the misrepresented present: where only the past is misguidedly thought to be relinquished. This belief of the world persists until its awkwardness is finally revealed as unsustainable within the realizations of a far-distant coming.

Through new thinking imposed upon the participants by the observable and chilling shifts of its environments, as an inevitable consequence of the old, ill-conceived choices of mindfulness imposed upon the world for so long, the environment begins its stabilizing response in scale as a karmic, reckoning force ready to make its sardonic mark upon an obliging humankind as a fatefully twisting resurface of equilibrium.

~~

Human history can be considered the admittance of its original denial and the surfacing of humankind's pressing starting illiteracy manifested upon the symbolic landscape of the preceding heeded universe. Consequences of denial, on a bodily and spiritual level, over layering generations atop generations of mostly choiceless identity within manifold experiential outcomes, with captured risks absolved through an initiated, conditioned psyche imprisoned by the parameters of its successes; and the quiet regression of its sensitivities through the shift of its skills in favor and inarguably capitulated to the sole domesticated mystification within humanity's rightfully asserted mortality and reclaimed otherworldly adventures.

Nature is forgiven its prior eminence within the human being, giving it the strength and vigor, the soundness of emotive certitude and proper deliberation, the behavioral routines of belief, and the conviction of solution within itself to stand alone as the intrinsic value of reality, as the fit arrival through the shedding of evolutionary consequences, and proudly admit to its tamed spiritual being as the gifted spiritual, emotive and mindful reality within its scope of the universe.

The consequences of choiceless spirituality, absolved of doubt or further embellishment, into a world of pure confidence of belief in what has been handed down by exhausted generations of temporal triumphs and prides. The current present state is restrained in its spirituality by the incomprehensible array of unprovable, symbolic beliefs of one overly reinterpreted environment acting in conflict through the confidence of localized elucidations being the emblems redeeming humankind's ongoing choices.

This current, presently unkempt state of the world stretching back most of the spans of millennia, should be conceivable proof of the failure of spiritual value rather than any measure of furthering success. This should demand an evolutionary shift in overcoming by embracement the antiquated origins of spirituality and its embedded imprint as a regressive outcome for promoting the physical manifestation of humanity as the inevitable, singular self-image of a world founded on disobedient thoughts and unetched beliefs claimed as truth.

In this thinking, there is no regard for the absences and voids of nature in store as sustenance for the emotive thinking, the patterns of meaning, and the symbols of belief for future generations condemned to nonexperience of nature's confidently enlightening essence. The condition of humanity's future becomes shaped by a world absent of natural context, of natural association, of shortened prose and creative backdrop for art, and without the natural world's insightful cues and hints furthering scientific discipline.

Instead, an impending barren creation is proffered and handed over as the chosen world like an ornately framed vacant landscape, inherited through the consequences of prior generational collusion of wild, vindicated inaction and the degradation of further incoming meaning or natural whispering for the future of probable solutions due to a willful efficiency and consuming fulfillment of the past finally absent of other than human spiritual awareness in an idyllic, lastly realized present state.

We reason our growing social evolution through methods mimicking the evolutionary struggles of nature. Both are made from the same stuff of reality, whether genetically inherited or relatedly sought and experienced.

Choices force a retainment of consequences, but consequences also force a retainment of eventual enforced choices. Consequences restrict and coerce future choices of entire populations of individuals with genetic reverberations gauging its outcoming realizations, regulating the intricacy of successes in advancing a future niche certainty for offspring to emerge into as a concreted world of human dominance atop a diminished world freed of natural experience, including a new humankind emotively attached to utter spiritual nonexistence as an inheritable, mystical enlightenment.

The risk and reward stratagem of evolution, niche compositions, degrees of conscious use, and the consequences of excessive choice upon a species of nature can be its undoing or its success in a skillful universe. Realizable choices are limited and unemotionally bound to the consequences of all prior choices and the resulting behaviors they reap no different than an identical genetic brand and held memory within each cell of a body, and the behaviors set by this vigorous confinement of alternatives pressed against its defining fate.

~~

It is a rebellious and unfounded envisioning of a reality where the individual walks a world and existence absent of justifying, inborn consequences in poised unison with other individuals, without the surfaced rewards of fraudulent personalities, transgressive leaders and privileges as representations, where the highest rewards of humanity are profitably accumulated by the basest, dominating and intimidating talents rather than its many more substantive aptitudes and remoter experiences of reciprocal human and nonhuman distinction as evident belief worthy of undergoing collective action and fitting inaction, and the higher behavioral adjustments required of unbiased ambitions.

These isolated individuals can be readily imagined existing in a far distant past, capable of extreme feats of perceptual connectedness as precursor to an acclaimed spiritual possessiveness to come later. They were emotionally attached to the natural world through a nonhuman bond with a textured, lushly pliable and survivable world, possessed of the memories at the newfound wonder of unprecedented events and the blossomed spectacle of reality to observe as isolated spiritual individuals consensually standing fully upright, heads cast upward eying the reflecting universe without alternate purpose or fitting design upon it beyond the moment of sensitive, absorbing observation.

An existence acts in mutual isolation and attachment alongside its living manifestations. This removal of natural freedom is given for collective benefit not the advantage of those simply willing and enabled by the prior forces raising its reality to do violation against fathomable weaknesses in others as an intimidating service to its immeasurable self-fulfillment.

Importantly, what a portion of these other violated individuals will not commit, out of consequence for reasons of integrity or the furthering of spiritual success and example, perpetuates the erosion of the best markings of humanity into a weakness and subjugation absent its required forcefulness due a necessitated mindful appeasement of an old, sympathetic conscience of nature.

Remnants of these old feelings will endure and haunt sensitively prone individuals. During any one time, there can be convinced persons to see more accurately their present and predict an inevitably mounting future to greater depth of vision.

During any past eras, rare persons will come to detectably view the impotence of a current knowledge in transition as limited in its ability to attain an answer with any immediacy within any of the countless, enamored present conditions of reality. They foresee a future in which the solution might be grasped. They must forcibly live and die without reaching a convincing meaning. Instead, they must exist as a waypoint along a path towards impending meaning for others to inevitably claim. Only in the dignity of humility can they reach a meaning to be found as an absence during their lifetime epochs.

And to view all around the mocking illusions of shadowed meanings in unavoidable, prismatic fruition, each demanding to prove itself the spiritual actuality of celestial perpetuity.

Without certainty, the sole redemption becomes the contrived and imaginable, or succumbing to the localized guesswork of nearest faith and its belief in a sensitivity of inner reality as the path towards any enlightenment of continuance beyond death.

This alluring treat of redemption becomes of utmost importance to the newfound consciousness of humanity it contrastingly existed without during the millennia of growth alongside nature's nonhumanity as a mere attribute of something phenomenal in its occurrence. This amazement happened within a universe only managing to divulge and excrete the methods of substantiality and the appearance of life atop a spinning globe within a relative infinity of observable reality.

~~

There are consequences of human actions, choices of morality, conflicts of belief, and exhaustive opportune reasons for abuse perpetrated upon nonhumanity and its senses, beliefs, emotive thought processes and survivability as continued evolutionary solutions.

As our knowledge and advancement grows, so too does nonhumanity evolve alongside us in findable spaces of attentions, perceptions and sensitivities when it comes to an increasingly fractured natural world it must often navigate without the full comforts of its niche selection and former accumulated successes providing it full stature and confidence. As environments shift, species become more victimized by lost niches, making of nature a collection of misshapen, unfit scavengers for the last bits of attentive reality before the fading awareness is gone due the overwhelming, dominant successes of a chokingly original, unidentifiable, insensate environment.

The human world becomes compounded by the risks of external threat and the unknown the same for all species within the natural world, and by the same standards of bravery or cowardice while evolving before it.

Recognizing our capabilities as a species, as measurements of accidental self-realization, without being perceptive to our capacities as a psychological invention of nature or the heedless reshaping of reality according to an image, as solitary remaining deliberation of a fate, our good fortune is lying behind and ahead in potential and range as an evolving exponential threat to the natural world and the achievement of its overwhelming prior feats becoming overwhelmingly lost, or at best unwittingly shifted to a distant, more hospitable, temporal future to convergently reoccur.

~~

The deniability of generations not collectively standing up against human history as an atrocious, *diagnosed* place, yet persistent in force in the present state of the world exactly the same as it always has been since the birth of our original ignorance began seeking the myriad truths hidden inside reality waiting to be challenged.

Learning to avoid admittance, through strategy of acceptance, of the consequences of actions and inactions, so that deeds can be more willfully done, so that an unfettered humanity can be less informed in its fitful becoming, unburdened by the implications of a lacking integrity as a gifted future.

A world where becoming an identity is a willful choice of being a singular human being, rather than the many forceful alternatives coerced by the circumstances of appalling outside constraints, due to other wills less restrained in choice of actions and behaviors, constrained now not by nature but by the preestablished surreal world of humanity as preeminent value.

To make a wasted misuse of human history contained as the embodiment of current disciplines of human achievement wrought through eons of delightful, restricting punishments for the betterment of stemming the emotively freeing world of ideas from enthusiastically billowing.

No species, with an aim of achieving enlightenment or anything resembling a goal or purpose, ever acts alone but in conjunction with all species within the present and its evolutionary history as a planet within a universe starved and longing for the recognizing discovery of meaning, rather than the exclusive sightlessness of its continuing absence.

Though currently eminent in its self-status, humanity is not a monopoly of thought, feeling or consciousness. We are simply a present time and place along the advancing lineage of this one planet. We are unsolicited other than through the accidental choice of our bodily shape and mental design, one meant inevitably to appear.

We are much less chosen by an omnipotence than we are designed and naturally evolved by the forces of the universe into a bodily shape, mind and environment, as a chance at singular enlightenment, where the true individual becomes a dynamic enthusiasm spotted in immeasurable space meant to hide it, alongside and the same as all other species in unbiased commonality, counted among the countless attempts at experience, the multiplicity of budding illumination and inklings of lighted, emotive amazement as living, grounded, and placed beings within a boundless cosmos fortuitously rooted in evolutionary actions of reality.

4. The Encouraging Deniability of Belief

The confidence of spiritual redemption in this world and an otherworld is the certainty of our opinions in action and physically crafted through the gifted elucidation of the human edifice, a world planned by human reworking, raised by the breaking toil of its demanded reality, with the proof of its solutions as iconic ranks and presumptive ideas as have been judged worthy of approved representations through the astuteness of humankind's vivid reason and especially emotive sense of awareness.

There can only be redemption following a path of humankind's ideas and sensitivity to ideas, since the connotation arises solely through the establishment of human supremacy navigating the diverging paths of truths, occurring above nonhumanity's tacit subjugation, as it has been practiced and stated to be the utmost vindication of the world and its celestial associations. Nature is helpless against the rousing voice of humankind.

No monopolized redemption of spiritual apparatus before existed in the world until the upright postured human being with its freshly shaped cranium permitted the revelation of its spirituality to be the awaited context of worldly reality since the beginning of the universe; as it became coincidently alleged, crowed on by its bulky mystical endowment, and thereby divulged with outrageous realization over the most recent millennia as humankind's burden to seek to fulfill.

Original scatterings of humankind carried it with them from the forests, waters and the mountains: the feeling of one whispering spirituality. Wherever it became an occurrence, humanity proved the same one, redefined, reimagined idea of unworldliness founded on its original emotive instinct for nature distortedly refocused upon its own conscious self-image through advancing its imaginative investigations of a strange new world.

Inevitably, it gained by revelation a visualized self-origin in coincidence with time and the universe given the confusing characteristic of unpracticed, infinite and newfound awarenesses of mind and emotive devotions of storied accounts.

With ample generational space within which to act, permitting it to focus and configure similar essential spiritual and humanized embodiments of a newly founded rightful place and consequence of the universe miraculously unveiled, this mysticism of mind struggled with an abrupt boundlessness of everything concerning mind and reality tempting its inclinations and believability. The only limits of this abrupt announcement of infinity are the restraints of its universal forces and the evolvement of its local environments anchoring it to the finite as a fixture of moveable appearance.

~~

Something, such as a simple symbol, which has meaning to one individual or group is likewise meaningless to another to the point of being worth the usefulness of posturing, intimidation and violence in matters of safeguarding the spiritual blood of life, even when the intended spirit is merely two portrayals of an equivalent value of meaning, of the same exceptional, peculiar interpretation of a physical and mystical environment.

The meaning of the world has been understood by interpretation throughout history, with dissimilar cultural and murmured articulations of the same emphasis of reality worthy of impassioned rallies, fighting for and against the impassioned rallies of others as a nurtured instinctual imitation of nature's superficiality of physical fitness in choiceless engagement due the shaped limitations of bodily challenges.

~~

In transcending this life as factual, there cannot be one truly lasting, dominant, favorite species. The path of one is the incorrect path of another, with equal validity like a particle's identified wave and pointed reality as multiplicity.

Embedded within humankind's ideas and emotional interpretations, as with nature as fitted niches within overall diverse environments, there must be a communal of philosophies like traits and sensual communications woven as a bionetwork by its species and inhabitants in conjunction and as accidental coincidence of willful unification. The ideas must be organized into a cohesive gathering of trait-like functions and sensitivities for the entirety of an environment atop a planet meant to evolve a means of genuine survival ranging a temporal moment and a singular placement within that moment.

Nature is devised of many environments filled by species through established niches acting as a unified force of betterment, and true individuality restrained to the wholeness of species as an entirety without superiority of a singular environment, or the overawing dominance of a master species of nature considered sufficiently attentive, intentional and willful in its penetrating designs.

~~

Redemption is not surrender, acceptable avoidance or inaction as an inner premeditated temperament embodied as resentful or embraced sightedness of the identified weaknesses of a vast humanity and nonhumanity vulnerable to its ploy. This detachment from the rest of reality occurs without deliberation of contrary sensitivities and awarenesses due the condition of biased localized surrealists preying upon environments as dominating predators.

Any true concept of redemption in individual and species is not forgetting the motives and locations of mountains, trees, waters and stars as valued and intrinsic to the whole, as consequence and source of any fitting spirituality and alleged chance at either enlightenment or forgiveness.

Redemption of individual and species does not have to be an attribute of reality. The universe continues with or without the encouragement of human or nonhuman evolvement.

Redemption involves admitting the circumstance of the compelling unknown, of an impending, approaching future valued with attention as a reoccurring equilibrium. This lacking advanced identification of our spiritual and physical manifestations clumsily cast in inanimate stone, iron and wood is our collectively mimicked, approving cheer for humankind.

This occurs alongside a life-force and universe capable of congealing an original sterile planet into an advancing thickness of proven evolvement and brimming environments justified by a success within each cell of each currently acting species among multitudes in improvement over a duly diminished past.

Few individuals truly find and indulge the species in such feelings of redemption, since few individuals can conceive or possess the power of prediction, imagination, and the confidence to view the species and world as a chronological wholeness through innumerable times and spacial locations exhausted by the cycled nature of life's shared existence.

As history and knowledge is progressively uncovered, what becomes revealed is humanity alone in an incomprehensible universe far beyond its understanding in scope throughout its succinct history. History proves humankind as a verging threshold of something imaginably higher within itself while perpetually conflicted by the manifold divine ideas of this interpreted imagination as an endless conflict over an originating spirituality taken from nature as a derivation; then compounded through scale of unlimited inexperience, collected metaphors and amassed events of dissociated histories.

Similar to how evolution can permit branching from an originating species into new similar and eventually dissimilar species afforded by prevalent conditions for new niche realizations, human spirituality has spread through wide and collapsing distances, its roots of origin from the same highlighted world, with its fluctuating environments of shapeshifted mysticisms, and abruptly exposed as a plaything to new localized versions of an adroit consciousness with pre-embedded tendencies of instinctive superstitions.

~~

Inevitably, with closing expanses of knowledge and growing successes of strategy, a new world will have to progressively admit the old world was never real due to its misrepresentations of physical and spiritual natures, yet its meaning remains within present reality as a hindering deniability falsely existing in disbelief of its own confusing reality rather than rightfully nostalgic and listening.

Eventually, it would be recognized and accepted through the growth of admittance to telling physical and spiritual natures to be the propagation of ideas, myths, human-made facsimiles of intentionally misunderstood human-specific meaning, taken in symbolic mockery from an all-encompassing natural world for the purpose of retreating from an unadmitted origin.

Instead, reimagining a new world where all the base spiritual motivations for human action are absent, where human spirituality is not the epitome of realizations within an endless universe, and all choices of the past and present abruptly become primarily empty of value other than human dominance of an environmental reality for its befitting purposes.

The honest measure of deniability and what it can achieve as behaviorisms and beliefs finds its countenance through the advent and incomplete surfacing of a certainty in human supremacy and this resource of spirit as motivating justification for any alleged consequences of stratagem and a relinquished demand for the final challenge of an endgame won either in this world or the locally accepted rendering of an otherworld.

Many beliefs are insubstantial and carry no true weight within the believers they each solely inhabit since the unprovable beliefs defy physicality, supporting the provision of meeker explanations and an appeasing attention to toil.

True belief in action according to true value surfaces within reality as something unnatural, anarchistic and selfishly recovered through self-sought resistance to a normalized world of meeker explanations.

Deniability becomes defeatism juxtaposed as success in the surreal world, with accompanying surrender of mind and the renunciation of the world for the absurd sake of an approved, otherwise unidentified, unchallenged self-meaning in an otherwise cold, uncentered universe.

~~

Baser sentiments are a regressed revilement against truer natures of being, or the distortions of humankind's idea of its spirituality started from a premeditated, far distant beginning, perpetuated through ensuing generations of history into a conviction.

Since the multitudes throughout history must accept any betrayal of nature whether against human or nonhuman, including delicately shocking actions concocted against fellow members of species, they cannot accept a gentler, contrary sentiment to emotively consider without admitting themselves possessed of the unfocussed conscience of a perpetrator. Some within this accumulation of peoples and long ages come to think themselves as a truer nature, as the agents of the physical and spiritual fireworks of this existence, adorning in this honor before the cosmos as a justification for means to an end action.

In earlier epochs, life was shorter in which to seek survival and occasional enlightenment as self-attempt at a wholeness of experience. Enlightenment as redemption is envisioned as denial of experiential countenance, as inner self-reflection contained as a constancy uninhibited by the reception of opinions from the outside world.

The birth and origin of the rare individual seeking spiritual denial of all prior attempts to self-disclosure by the species becomes healthily contrasted against the skilled, popular creeds of humankind's idolized spirituality.

~~

Human beliefs, like all else human beyond instinctive physiology, as a recent phenomenon within the world or, through an extreme of imaginative potential, the entire cosmos, is not fully instinctual but cultured beyond any genetic resistances to contexts of environments and histories of differentiated experiences consuming a prior confidence in nature while instilling its own brand of sureness.

There are varied, manifold states of aware, wavelike realities based on species, the forces and symmetries of existence, niche-consumed localities and embedded, structural environments, histories and directions of evolutionary choice among a preestablished library of innovative and convergent solutions to reality's dilemmas contained as an impression of a world and its envisioned universe atop a compulsively whirling bubble ensnarled by and as the symbol of one kind of sought existence.

As with a writer creating a book of fiction, word by word, line by line, and chapter by chapter consumed with emotive ideas, the experiential familiarity creating the words is the latency of existence, there waiting to be shaped, limited in potentiality by disinformed beliefs as difficult to disentangle as reality itself in all its immense and spirited pride of composed associations defining the solutions of celebrated species like ancient tomes of great, mastered art.

~~

By a peculiar twist of belief agreed from past ages, humankind as the spiritual epitome of the universe transcends in death rather than in life. Death becomes the alleged source of measurement of a feared justice.

No one species such as human beings, being an embryonic, willful origin of nature, could possibly transcend the universe, the world, nature, or enlightenment into deathful permanence founded on self-purpose or self-glorification without true merit of disbelief and strategy of denial. Yet, as an appeasement of the senses and imaginations, it becomes the roots of environmental becoming within the human realm of physical transcendence into spiritual being as the spoken beginning of honored networks of belief.

It would be more pressing and fitting to see the act of existing within a complicated reality as the enlightenment to shadow and aspire. By the design of the universe, the value surfacing from destruction usually must precede the pursuit in intended imitation, otherwise there is no original conception to follow and seek like the lure of a tempted soul plainly imprisoned within a transgressed body awaiting the awakening of mortality as choice for reprieve into wholeness.

Within the realms of complex potentialities and forceful evolutionary compulsions required of an especially sensitive conscious spirituality, this belief can lead and imperil an entire world of ideas as it pursues, as overwhelming stratagem, an unsuspecting future confounded by true, surreal beliefs as mentor in the detection of intended actions and the designed, mystical asylums for appeasing the long intimidating anticipation of a welcoming afterworld.

This method of stating the world enables and empowers the non-believing, non-spiritual, non-empathic potentials of a talented humankind due an aged, embedded design found to act supreme and as a fitting success of posturing, embattled actors upon the world and representation of humanity and nonhumanity as its answering, scripted stage drama before the celestial audience.

~~

Morality as normalcy cannot take true, natural spirituality out of the equation into something wholly human, any more than it can be gauged in its associations to solely human idyllic endeavors of heroism and confident devotion without the success-woven conviction for nature's nonhuman world existing alongside.

The proportionalities of human progress are built on the endurance of now-labelled, categorized and normalized disorders as attentive connotations of truth, of spiritual-minded individuals forced to suffer and quietly divulge a contradictory perception of normalcy, as entertaining human mysticisms of spiritual instigation, and strange practices of manifold ceremonial beliefs in a common, current state during any of the apportioned past's many located states of innovative devotions. These shifting spiritualities attempt to persevere on some level for the betterment of others, especially the future as an only endowment of self-assessment during an individual lifetime without motivating affection for its meandering afterworld.

The only solution becomes to be motivated in belief by reality and its prismatically announced, communicating description.

Instead, the alternative is a caricature of human invention trying to highjack that same naturalness of belief in existence with compulsive, indulgent aims. A mind and body must be attuned in empathy with reality as its reflection, not through glorification or the mimicking impulse of sacrifice and fear; but through deliberate vision and instinct of individuals among collectives and a wonderment at its endorsed celestial and pulsing actuality.

~~

Human history has been excessively restrained by the justifications for choices and behaviors left for the future to divulge, an abusive consequence of the polluted idea that an unlived, unfelt eventual future ends will justify the means of present actions as a lopsided equating of a symmetrical reality, as if such consequences were predetermined, ordained and not merely imagined in fullness by and for the involved participants of an astounding, divinely rapt species.

Generally, no one has the capability to solely predict even the near, local future by current actions with much accuracy or depth of honest confidence, becoming further encouraged to ruin the longer the attempted prediction seeks beyond the immediacy of a fleetingly stabilized, replenished moment.

~~

The disinformation of humanity goes back to as far as the beginning of its rapport as a malleable consciousness, beyond the first tools embedding images on stone. It starts at an origin extending outward to the present state of the world. All divergent successes are ignored as unbefitting unless of disclosed usefulness as an imitating ploy, forced and constrained by the environment's composition and a past filled with funneling, believable selections.

The impulses motivating conscious minds are multifaceted and range the far recesses of potentials in its seeking after itself as a proper meaning, enlightenment, niche or divine origin; but the atrocious extortion is the same in all debasement, in each surrendering self-belief, in the resentful futility of acting as an individual against stacked odds of finding genuine, confirmed accountability of spiritual rewards within the vast range of physical validations.

The spirit of reality is the invention of a limited opinion of reality exposed through human doubts, inhibitions, fears and uncertainties exemplified in the surrounding environment its consciousness awoke within as an originally proud, expectant confidant of nonhuman nature.

This prided original being had been fitted as a deity for the natural world. As an accumulation of belief in the unification of all species, and the certainty of its emotive insights, its beginning sightedness instead oddly redirected upon a mirroring reflection of its spiritualized personification as sole embodiment of the universe and the embedded epitome of perfected, long-sought answer.

5. Survival of the Fittest?

Finding within a species the wholeness of its physical and mystical natures as defining fitness can be conceived as the embodiment of any individual entity's niche-embedded manifestation, its evolving, grouped connectivity of merged awarenesses attuned with the imbued suggestions of its bodily sensitivities; and its success of enthrallment at the overawing, commanding experiences of contended niche discipline.

Fitness is the survival of environments and the innovated diversity essential to its pronounced wholeness through an interwoven multiplicity of workable species. Fitness goes beyond genetics to collective unities of shifting interactions within conflicting, predatory and attentive environments of excessive, ploy-filled commotion.

Fitness is the survival and flourishing originations of wide-ranging selected, successful functions, convergent within reality as all species' aptitude for finding, devising and understanding niches. Fitness is manifold enhancement and communicative awarenesses sighted through these niches and the embodying environments they jointly reap as coinciding origin.

Fitness is not fixed in time and space, but malleable, transitional, reliably changeable to adaptations through the goings-on of its endless momentum of succeeding, roving species. Fitness is the natural cycle of unsuccessful species replaced by the redeploying evolvement of others within fluctuating, moveable environments.

Fitness is the skilled maneuverability of species balancing an undulating equilibrium with compound dimensionalities of acting solutions in common as an overwhelming allowance for postured, described robustness.

Fitness is the thriving control restraining overly dominant populations from successes over the course of a world's entirety until a precariously uncontrolled present state of concentrated momentum.

~~

An impulsive human species finds itself empowered to regulate and manage nature for its benefits but does not apply equal regulation in its constraints on well-resourced human populations as a wellspring of proper fitness due a habituated denial of future outcomes. This lack of concerning attention ensued from eons of finding the limitlessness of the world and its veracious, enabling appetite for consumption of humanity's waste as enthusiastically as nature's thickening lushness hides all truths of the past.

As survival appeasement for a distressed emotive mind, fitness as a history of humankind is furthest to the centered path and closest to extremities of reality's explorations, balancing between the advancements of opposing systems of hatred to the point of overcoming the vital, artful trials of humanity's painstaking struggle for physical and spiritual resolution without acknowledging the long-ago abandonment of its further journey.

~~

Survival of the fittest is not a competition of species but of niche developments and allotments, since the transformations of physicality through the evolution of species is mainly cosmetic and trivial other than for the apportionments of traits, bodily shapes and perspective awarenesses as a defined acting compilation of directed skills within a vibrating, feedbacking environment of otherwise vacated niches.

If a species loses its local rivalry, surrendering its niche due to environmental change or victimized by the overwhelming success according to the outside arrival of a competing trait against which it cannot find adaptation, the potential and actuality of the niche still exists in the same or other localities and within other future species as a closely cooperative interpretation of temporal reality convergently sprouting.

Only a barren, spiritless, exploited and benign worldly environment with an absence the niche affordances, or consumed by unafforded niche relics, makes of evolution a quieted absence with a remote, unimproved latency of unadorned occurrence.

No species dominates all others since none in advanced bodily shapes can exist for long in isolation from other species unless within a world inhospitable to all but the least of life's limits.

Without a new environment to slink into and develop alongside, evolution stops affording isolation from other species as niches in competition for an overall resounding fitness of an overarching environmental triumph; a solution much like the world as it transpired over the bulk of its evolving history until wrought by the growing seductions of the recently present, old world of humankind.

~~

Humanity's fitness can be tricky, purposefully misdirecting, opportune, appeasing for denial, and willfully lacking in acceptance of the unacceptable. It can occur as the observance of an embraced, deluded identity of species as favored of carnal successes. Localized surrenders can be expected, but with each relinquishment of nature is enhanced an intentional involvement towards future offspring trained by the winning aptitudes of the consumed past.

Reciprocally, the fitness of all species evolves into environmental fitness, so that what was in the past becomes something new in the present as an overall spectrum of fitness for living assortments of species.

This genetically carved fitness restraining a species to its new, obsessively focused worldly viewpoint without alternative can inescapably transform into a colony or hive-like behaviorism not originally envisioned, achieved through the straining overexertion of the genetically prescribed capacities of its bodily shape, creating unfit, adverse genetic and behavioral repercussions on a temporal scale, inclusive of near-reaching futures sullied by the favor of past winning strategies no longer applicable as sustainable, livable choice confronting a shifted spectrum of worldly movement.

~~

Fitness is not a singular species likened in the eyes of nature and universe, but likened compilations of adaptations, likened diversity of traits, and likened spanning, overlapping environments of shared obligations.

Environments can migrate under subtle or abrupt change to larger environmental shifts, though not with the same rapid urgency of transitioning traits among all species of plant and animal accorded stratagems of survival, and the ensuing struggle can be much like a drought of evolutionary changeover and loss of adaptability within its violently textured array of equilibrium provisioning a freshly balancing state of worldly poise intended as austere breeding grounds for all except the fittest of the rapidly-changeable fit.

Entire species become reduced, delimited in success by the accomplishment of rapid external change upon the disconnected shifting of so many environmental niches wildly panicking in unison like a silent, agonizing scream of fitted bewilderment.

The exiling surrender of a world of individuals among countless species reduced to niche scavengers searching newly fading environments for revisions to skills no longer relevant, and the increasing absence of useful skills due to an evolutionary imitation of the devolving environment. These collective species exist as if escaped from their niche cages into existential surrender, starved and choked by the new, empty reality of the scattering, de-evolutionary breakage of diversity.

Species, for the first instance and without solicitation, begin to rapidly catch up with humanity in the forceful discovery of a detached nature and the festival of conscionable nihilism as a new, unquestionable mode of truth.

~~

This level of enabled dissolution exists within the spectrums of politics, economies and entire collectives of peoples exhibiting this same resolution as an overwhelming unfitness to worldly longevity and the dominating winners of one species above everything true, alive, thoughtful or emotive, as an endgame of provable waste as the scales of ecstatic consciousness, as mocking pleasures at the environment's surrender of its iconic values to human spiritual consumption for the sake of the transitory fitness of succeeding personalities, identities, and dissolving beliefs during a brief measure of celestial appearance; as an endowment of the universe ready and provisioned with the means to succeed or be overwhelmed by its far-reaching ideas.

A world can be raised to victimize its unbeknownst inhabitants. To describe oneself honestly in such a world is to describe the honors of a prey costumed inside the ready predatory traits of a donning collective personality with quantified, monetized talents of valued survivability.

Nature had to skillfully overcome all the embryonic complications of evolution for so long, balancing the convergent reoccurrences shaped by the fingers of universality, the consequences of past choices infiltrated and filtered through innumerable solutions forced into innovative continuations embedded by species. Nature awoke from a self-designed world far removed from any other in proximity or scale within the reach of light, and to far greater depth of insight and description of reality than any challenge it in turn presented to humanity and the nonhuman world with deft, imaginative and affording vision.

~~

Fitness can smoothly enact and enable the acceleration of an opinionated persuasion of originally unsolicited dominance upon the world as a growing force in need of revolting against as a rule of nature. Reciprocally, fitness of awarenesses can pronounce a counter world of empathic equilibrium, dependent upon past and present chosen paths of believable acceptances and appeasement for an advancing, weaning mainstream.

Fitness belongs to the species and individuals to predict their future accurately, acting upon it within scales of proportionality and observances of later potentials as a promoted niche dominance: a difficult fitness to support in an otherwise mute reality encouraging self-realization.

This fitness has been repeated throughout history in limited spaces gradually coming together and joining into a single fitness ripe for directed solutions of its own contriving insights. This diversity of species is fit to formulate a world attuned to its iconic marks of self-interpretation in sequestered absence from the quieted universe, absent from minded contacts with forces of life minimalized by one chosen pride marked as master and fiefdom over a worldly entirety.

If success comes from the conquerable, there would be no diversity of the natural world. Nature would have already found this solution. It is the believability stemming from the original temporal ignorance of an advancing consciousness for a random species to mistakenly claim itself the originating solution over a world's lasting future as the new, chosen arrival.

~~

There are individuals to see the feeling of existence and consider the futility of striving for dominance within a reality, of trying, caring, searching and enduring for the sake of a supposed, illusive meaning. They feel the barbarous intent of an unobserving, empty reality founded on nothing more than fabricated perspective of a world hardly penetrated in its unequalled depths.

Finally, after enduring eons of evolved agony, these individuals arrive into a world asking and teaching the question, with sympathetic inflection, as to why a biosphere would strive the agonies of evolution for eons to produce a singular species for its spiritual meaning in the otherwise emptiness of a cold universe, to become this means to an end as an instinctive, amusing wonderment at survival's final product.

Surviving because of a landscaped reality, established as a surreal reality of identity as both master and slave together like particle and wave permeating humanity's reassurances, without the primal peace among species afforded by nature's prior forceful boundaries, nature does have its tolerances, rewards and detrimental pitfalls accorded the designing ambitions of any singular species.

Survival of a species to no end other than the idea of its own dominant physical and spiritual natures as servicing justness and self-claimed enlightenment for the sake of no better aiming invention of imagination, scrubbed from the prior environments of succeeding betterment, humankind has supplanted the integrity of natural subsistence in favor of the instinctiveness of economic survival as a divine sacrifice attained through excruciated flailing of the originating, spirited nonhuman and human realms.

~~

Human aptness opened new avenues of exploration for complex environmental fitness, for new potentialities in combination with a dexterous bodily shapeliness surfacing from the multifaceted world of unconscious, attaching encouragement; perpetrated instead into a wildly celebrated, rebellious, primal scream at an attempted echo as response, a familiarly self-willed, unanswered resounding as an otherwise mute proof against celestial certainty.

For a singular species existing on a planet without capability of reaching another, alone in a universe without direct contact with anything further within an infinity other than streams of venerable light, and allowing its world to deteriorate, for the manifold species of its planet to swiftly exodus from existence into dust, for future generations to miss the opportunity of existence on exhibit atop a planet in an existing, awing universe, would seem a reasonably questionable sort of fitness newly explored as an ambitious origination of innovative reality.

Manufactured by Amazon.ca
Bolton, ON